AN ILLUSTRATED HISTORY OF
MILITARY MOTORCYCLES

AN ILLUSTRATED HISTORY OF
MILITARY MOTORCYCLES

100 YEARS OF WARTIME MOTORCYCLES, FROM THE FIRST MACHINES OF WORLD WAR I
TO THE DIESEL-POWERED TYPES AND QUAD BIKES OF TODAY, WITH 230 PHOTOGRAPHS

PAT WARE

southwater

This edition is published by Southwater
an imprint of Anness Publishing Ltd
Blaby Road, Wigston
Leicestershire LE18 4SE
info@anness.com

www.southwaterbooks.com
www.annesspublishing.com

Anness Publishing has a new picture agency outlet for images for publishing, promotions
or advertising. Please visit our website www.practicalpictures.com for more information.

© Anness Publishing Ltd 2012

A CIP catalogue record for this book is available from the British Library.

Publisher: Joanna Lorenz
Senior Editor: Felicity Forster
Cover Design: Nigel Partridge
Production Controller: Steve Lang

Produced for Anness Publishing by JSS Publishing Limited
Editor: Jasper Spencer-Smith
Designer: Nigel Pell
Editorial Assistant: Lizzie Ware
Copy Assistant: Maree Brazill
Scanning: Reaction Ltd, Poole BH12 1DJ

Previously published as part of a larger volume,
The World Encyclopedia of Military Motorcycles

PUBLISHER'S NOTE
Although the information in this book is believed to be accurate and true
at the time of going to press, neither the authors nor the publisher can accept any
legal responsibility or liability for any errors or omissions that may be been made.

PAGE 1: **Harley-Davidson, WL.** PAGE 2: **BMW R-35, 350cc, single cylinder.** PAGE 3: **Harley-Davidson, WLA.**
PAGE 4: **Suzuki LT125 4x4 quad bike.** PAGE 5: **Moto-Guzzi** *Trialce.*

Contents

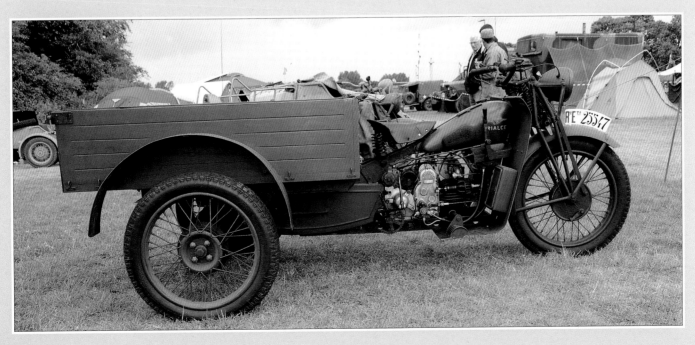

Introduction

The history of the military motorcycle dates back to the very beginning of military mechanization, and to the earliest days of the development of motorcycles. Soon after the close of the 19th century, Britain, Germany, and Austria had all started to acquire motorcycles for military use. By the time of World War I, other nations had also purchased their first military motorcycles as the machine began to be seen as a possible replacement for the horse.

However, clearly the military motorcycle could also be used in other roles. Back then, the "weapon of mass destruction" was the machine-gun. In Britain and Germany, in particular, tacticians realized that relatively small groups of soldiers could lay down withering barrages of fire using their weapons. What is more, the introduction of the motorcycle sidecar combination meant that machine-guns could become mobile. While it was not possible to fire on the move, at least not without considerable risk to other riders, firing parties could move rapidly from one position to another – what is known in military parlance as "shoot and scoot".

Not only did the motorcycle become technically more reliable during World War I, but also proved to be of tactical and logistical value. By the 1920s, the military motorcycle was a standard item in the inventory of most armies.

There had been experiments with armoured sidecars during World War I, and several nations also attempted to produce small armoured reconnaissance, and even offensive vehicles, using solo and combination motorcycles during the 1930s. Similarly, the addition of tracks to a motorcycle might improve cross-country capability but did little for cornering performance and the general dynamics involved in balancing a fast-moving machine on two wheels.

ABOVE: **A line-up of sidecar-equipped Harley-Davidsons of the US Motorcycle Corps photographed at Fort Brown, Brownsville, Texas. The machines have the standard civilian sidecar.**

In the years leading up to World War II, the Nazi government purchased thousands of motorcycles for military use. Amongst the combatant nations in the conflict, the *Wehrmacht* used more motorcycles for service with combat troops. Germany was also alone in commissioning large numbers of specialized military motorcycles as opposed to simply adapting existing civilian models. Indeed, the big BMW and Zündapp sidecar outfits of the *Kradschützen* probably remain the high point in the development of the military motorcycle.

Although Britain had experimented with machine-gun sidecars in the early stages of the war, the arrival of the US-built Jeep saw Allied use of the motorcycle reduced to the messenger role from around 1942.

The late 1940s, and the decades which followed, saw the military motorcycle being used in a relatively minor role, relegated to traffic control and convoy escort duties. Notwithstanding some experiments with automatic transmission, those machines purchased were frequently derived directly from civilian types. Indeed, so few military motorcycles were being procured across the world during the 1960s and 1970s that the Japanese "invasion" of the motorcycle market had little effect. During the 1980s and 1990s, military motorcycles were lightweight multi-terrain machines which could be used by reconnaissance troops or despatch riders. Others were stripped-down utility versions of the big civilian touring machines which could be used for convoy escort and military police work.

It is only in the last decade or so that the military motorcycle market has been rejuvenated by experience gained in the conflicts in Iraq and Afghanistan. Here, quad bikes and enduro-type off-road machines proved valuable in moving lightly equipped troops across difficult terrain. Perhaps the increases in size and weight of vehicles such as the HMMWV, and even the Land Rover, mean that Special Forces and clandestine units really need a new "Jeep" – and the quad bike and trailer is almost a Jeep. Finally, a recent joint UK/US project has seen the emergence of the first practical diesel-powered motorcycle.

The pages that follow detail the fascinating story of the use of the military motorcycle over more than 100 years. The introductory section looks at the role of the military motorcycle, the early pioneers, the anatomy of the motorcycle and the emergence of a standardized layout. The book then covers military motorcycles from World War I to 1939, followed by machines from World War II to the present day. There is also a country-by-country overview of military motorcycles in France, Belgium, Germany, Italy, Great Britain, the USA, the USSR and Japan, accompanied by photographs from all over the world.

ABOVE: **The *Wehrmacht* was an enthusiastic user of motorcycles of all sizes during the late 1930s and throughout World War II.** LEFT: **The multi-terrain Armstrong, later Harley-Davidson, MT350 and MT500 are typical of current military motorcycles.**

ABOVE: **The Harley-Davidson military Model J with the standard factory sidecar was widely used by US and Allied forces during World War I.**

The role of the military motorcycle

Before the advent of reliable radio communications and encryption techniques, the physical – or "ear-to-ear" – delivery of messages, orders, despatches, etc was a vital military function. At first runners were used for this purpose and, in time, horses supplanted the runners – Robert Browning's poem tells how the "good news" was brought from the Belgian city of Ghent to Aix by three riders, while in the previous century, Paul Revere's historic overnight ride from Boston to Lexington in 1775 told the rebels of the movements of the British Army.

As the motorcycle started to replace the horse during World War I, it seemed obvious that the horse-mounted despatch rider could simply be replaced by one riding a motorcycle. Given a degree of mechanical reliability, the mount would not succumb to fatigue – the rider was another matter altogether – and the motorcycle was able to negotiate cratered ground that would have caused the horse to throw its rider.

While despatch riding almost certainly was the first role for the military motorcycle and, nearly a century

ABOVE: **During World War II, the British Army tended to restrict motorcycles to the liaison and despatch role.** FAR LEFT: **The German Zündapp company produced the K500W from 1933 until 1940 and, although it was basically a civilian machine, it was widely used by the *Wehrmacht*.** LEFT: **The *Wehrmacht* was not always the epitome of mechanization – here Nazi infantrymen carry a pigeon basket on a lightweight motorcycle.**

later, remains a significant aspect of the use of these machines, it was not the only role.

The motorcycle also allowed reconnaissance and scouting units to penetrate into enemy territory. The first US soldier into Germany during World War I – Corporal Roy Holtz of Chippewa Falls, Wisconsin – was taking his captain on a reconnaissance mission in northern Belgium. The pair, riding a Harley-Davidson motorcycle, became lost and ended up asking for directions at a farmhouse, which they then discovered was being used as a German Army billet. Both were taken prisoner only to be released a couple of days later when the armistice was declared.

Attempts were also made to use motorcycles as a kind of mechanical cavalry and during World War I, the British, US and German armies all experimented with mounting a machine-gun on to a motorcycle, either using a specially adapted sidecar or by fitting the gun directly on to the handlebars. It was impossible to fire the thing on the move, at least with any hope of hitting anything, but nevertheless, motorcycles continued to carry machine-guns throughout World War II. In the mid-1950s, the French even tried to mount a recoilless anti-tank weapon on a scooter. The German heavy motorcycles of World War II were also designed to act as artillery tractors or to tow light trailers.

Medical evacuation was a particular problem during World War I and many motorcycles were fitted with ambulance or stretcher-carrier sidecars. While a bumpy ride on a primitive motorcycle across the rutted and shell-holed ground would not have been the first choice of any seriously wounded man, the alternative was probably to be left in a shell hole to die.

During World War II, ultra-light motorcycles were developed by Britain, America and Italy that could be air-dropped by parachute alongside airborne troops. Although the machines were slow and uncomfortable, they did at least provide instant mobility in the field. Other behind-the-lines roles included convoy escort duties, traffic control and military police work.

Today, no-one would dream of using a motorcycle combination as a regular means of transporting the wounded and, while guns might not be mounted on to motorcycles, there is every reason to believe that the quad bike lends itself well to such a role. The modern army has significantly fewer motorcycles, but in many other respects, surprisingly little has changed. The motorcycle continues to be used for despatch and courier duties, convoy escort work, traffic control, rescue missions behind enemy lines, reconnaissance, and in military police units. The mobility of the motorcycle remains its primary military advantage.

The motorcycle pioneers

There is a saying that "when the time comes to railroad, everybody railroads" and in the latter years of the 19th century there were sufficient attempts being made to build a powered bicycle to suggest that here was an idea whose time had come. The earliest machines were steam powered but, aside from the obvious safety issues for anyone sitting astride a firebox and a tank full of boiling water, there were practical considerations such as the problems of carrying, or finding, sufficient fuel and water for a journey of more than 24km/15 miles.

Steam-powered motorcycles never really became a practical proposition but the way forward came in the form of the internal combustion engine. In 1885, two German engineers, Gottlieb Daimler and Paul Maybach, fitted a 270cc four-stroke petrol engine into a largely wooden two-wheeled chassis that

ABOVE: **Although women had yet to be granted the right to vote, during World War I the shortage of men frequently found women doing what had traditionally been men's work. These uniformed women of a voluntary AID detachment are mounted on a selection of essentially civilian outfits.** RIGHT: **A US infantryman attends to his Indian Powerplus, a model introduced in 1917. Indian, Excelsior and Harley-Davidson quickly established themselves as the leading manufacturers in the USA.**

they called *Einspur* or *Reitwagen*, depending on your source. Despite its small stabilizer wheels, many consider this to be the world's first proper motorcycle.

In 1894, the Germans Hildebrand & Wolfmüller produced the first commercial motorcycle, a 1,488cc twin-cylinder machine which used rubber belt drive and was capable of 40kph/25mph. Only a few hundred were built and it was not a commercial success.

However, while the German engineers had proved that the manufacture of such a device was possible, it took a pair of Frenchmen, Count Albert de Dion and Georges Bouton to kick-start the motorcycle industry. In 1897, De Dion-Bouton offered their own engine for general sale. Initially with a capacity of 270cc but soon uprated to 500cc, the engine was licensed and copied across the world.

Meanwhile, the pedal cycle industry was in full swing in the years leading up to the turn of the 20th century and, by 1885, the frame and wheel layout devised by John Kemp Starley for his Rover "safety cycle" had become the norm. With its low centre of gravity, chain transmission and equal-sized wheels, the design lent itself well to being motorized, and the subsequent availability of reliable engines, persuaded many cycle builders to offer motorized versions of their products. Despite experiments that placed the engine over the rear wheel, behind the saddle, and even on a small trailer which pushed the machine along, it was clear that the best place for the engine was between the frame down-tube and the seat-tube, close to the ground. Thus was established the standard motorcycle layout.

As engines became more powerful, the design started to move away from its bicycle origins and features such as sprung forks and multi-speed transmissions started to appear. The number of manufacturers increased rapidly, and many of the companies that would be the big names

ABOVE: **The motorcycle is a Triumph Model H, but clearly safety was not a primary concern during these early years.**

of the industry for the next half century appeared in the years leading up to World War I.

The British company Scott produced their first motorcycle in 1898 and went into full production in 1908. Triumph and Ariel were both established in 1902, Velocette in 1904, and BSA in 1906. In France, Clement and René Gillet started motorcycle production in 1897 and 1898, respectively, and Peugeot began working on motorcycles in 1899. Terrot was established in 1901. The German company NSU made its first motorcycle in 1901, and Wanderer in 1902. Over in the USA, Carl Oscar Hedstrom and George I.M. Hendee had founded the Hendee Manufacturing Company in 1900. Their aim was to produce a "motor-driven bicycle for the everyday use of the general public". Within a year, they had produced the Single, a 1.75hp machine with a top speed of 40kph/25mph. By 1914, Hendee's Indian motorcycle had become the best-selling motorcycle in the world. Harley-Davidson, soon to take this title from Indian, first appeared in 1903.

By 1914, more than 720 motorcycle manufacturers had been established worldwide, albeit more than a few failed within a year or two of starting operations. But, when Europe went to war that year, for many soldiers it was astride a motorcycle.

ABOVE: **Motorcycles were quickly adopted for military use and were frequently seen as a direct replacement for the horse.**

ABOVE: **Sidecars were used to mount machine-guns and also to carry parts and ammunition. Some were fitted as stretcher carriers.**

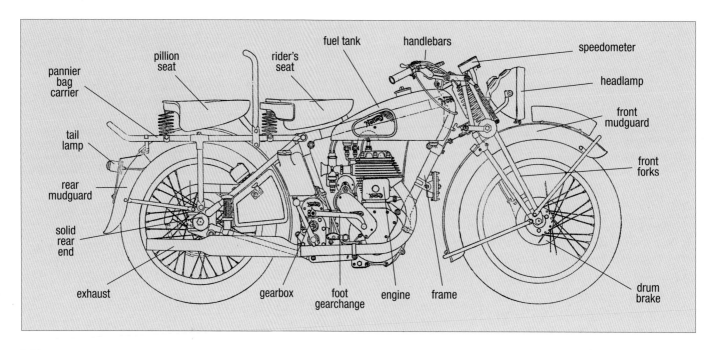

The anatomy of a motorcycle

In the early days, there was little consensus on how the various components of the motorcycle should be assembled with designers disagreeing over the details of engines, suspension, brakes and transmission.

Frame

Early motorcycles were constructed on a diamond-shaped tubular backbone frame similar to that used for pedal cycles. Until well into the 1950s, it was common to employ a single down-tube, but as the machines got heavier and engines got larger, paired wishbone shaped down-tubes of the duplex frame were required to provide a wider engine support.

External pressed-steel perimeter frames appeared during the 1930s, with the frame wrapping around the outside of the machine. In recent years this style has returned, now using square-section steel or aluminium tubing. Some modern machines use the frame tubes as an oil, or even fuel, reservoir.

Engine

Many of the pioneering manufacturers used proprietary engines – for example, the products of JAP, MAG, Villiers and Sachs.

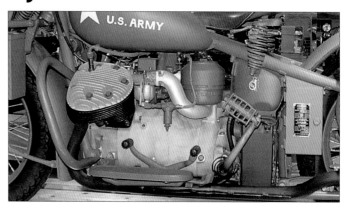

Side-valve or inlet-over-exhaust valve layout was common at first but by the early 1950s almost all machines were fitted with overhead valves. Two-strokes started to appear in the 1930s, and were particularly championed by DKW. Diesel power is extremely rare in motorcycles since the power characteristics of the engine do not really suit the performance required from a motorcycle.

Pre-war engines with a capacity up to 500cc were frequently of single-cylinder design but even from the early days, twin-cylinder arrangements were not uncommon, including V, horizontally opposed, side-by-side (parallel), and in-line configurations, while Ariel became famous for their four-cylinder square layout. Puch devised an unusual split-piston two-stroke using two pistons running in parallel cylinder bores, but sharing a combustion chamber, spark plug and cylinder head; one piston controlled the inlet ports, the other the exhaust. Modern motorcycles tend to be multi-cylinder design.

TOP, ABOVE AND LEFT: **Although there was plenty of room for eccentricity in design during the early years, a standardized motorcycle layout quickly emerged, and while the US favoured big V-twin engines (above), the single or twin-cylinder design (left) was more usual in Europe.**

Magneto ignition was common until the 1940s, but this was gradually replaced by the familiar battery and coil arrangement, and then by solid-state electronic systems.

Virtually all machines built before the 1980s were air-cooled, but water-cooling has become far more common.

Transmission

While the very earliest machines used a form of direct drive, a multi-speed gearbox is essential to exploit the torque and power characteristics of the engine. Initially installed separately, the gearbox was usually connected to the engine by an exposed primary chain. So-called "unitary construction" became more common from the 1930s, whereby the gear train is incorporated in the engine castings.

Some early motorcycles had the gearbox in the rear hub, and some manufacturers have even experimented with automatic or stepless belt drive.

Final drive

The final drive connects the gearbox to the rear wheel. Many early machines used belt drive, either a flat leather belt, or a fabricated belt made from separate links. The big German BMW and Zündapp machines were notable for their use of shaft drive – in modern versions the shaft runs inside an oil bath in one of the rear fork legs, but on older machines the shaft was exposed. However, roller chains remain by far the most common form of drive.

ABOVE AND ABOVE RIGHT: **The girder parallelogram forks (left) remained the standard design until the end of World War II, when the telescopic pattern (right) began to be fitted.**

Front forks and suspension

The earliest front suspension consisted of parallelogram forks, with tubular girder or pressed-steel fork blades secured by short pivoting links to a pair of yokes at the steering head. The forks were cushioned against movement using one, or a pair of friction-damped coil springs between the top and bottom yokes or, less frequently, using a horizontal leaf spring. On leading link forks, the pivot points are at the bottom of the forks, with the centre of the wheel placed forward of the steering axis, but Indian and early BMW machines used a trailing link which placed the axle behind the steering axis.

These designs gradually gave way to the modern telescopic forks whereby the coil spring and damping mechanism are contained in a telescopic strut filled with hydraulic fluid.

Rear forks and suspension

Early motorcycles had no rear suspension at all, relying on a sprung saddle to insulate the rider from road shocks. From about the mid-1940s it became common to provide cushioned rear forks, most commonly using a trailing arm or hinged subframe suspended on a friction-damped coil spring; compressed rubber blocks or leaf springs have also been used. Plunger-type suspension was also common for a period, notably used by BMW and Ariel, where the forks remained fixed but the rear axle was allowed to move on coil-sprung vertical plungers.

Modern machines tend to use a trailing swing arm, often single-sided, suspended on a coil spring, which is damped by a sealed hydraulic shock absorber.

MIDDLE AND ABOVE: **Most motorcycles manufactured before 1945 had a rigid, unsprung rear end (middle). The standard rear end these days consists of a swing arm suspended on a telescopic unit (above).**

Brakes

It was not unusual at first to provide brakes only on the rear axle, frequently using a block acting directly on to the rim or on to either the belt-drive pulley or a dummy rim. Early front brakes were sometimes of the caliper design.

Since the 1920s, it has been standard practice to fit brakes at front and rear, at first using mechanically operated expanding shoes inside a drum, this gradually giving way to hydraulic operation. Modern practice is to use hydraulic disc brakes, front and rear.

A standardized layout emerges

These days, all motorcycles conform to a standardized layout – the engine nestles in the frame beneath the tank and drives the rear wheel via a clutch, unit-constructed gearbox, with final drive by chain or propeller shaft. The front and rear forks are both provided with damped suspension in the interests of road-holding and rider comfort. As regards controls, forward motion is controlled by a right-hand twist grip, and the gear change is operated via a foot pedal on the right side; a second pedal, on the left, is used to apply the rear brake. A hand lever on the right operates the front brake, a similar lever on the left operates the clutch.

It wasn't always thus. It took until 1914 for the standardized layout of frame, engine and transmission to appear – and by this time, the motorcycle had acquired its own set of design rules and had lost its early resemblance to the bicycle.

Notwithstanding the handful of brave manufacturers who chose to place the engine over the rear wheel, or even ahead of the front forks where it drove the front wheel, there was an early consensus on fitting the power unit low down in the frame, just above what would have been the bottom bracket on a conventional pedal cycle frame. Not only did this give the optimum centre of gravity, but it also made it relatively easy to get drive to the rear wheel. And the obvious place for the fuel tank was above the engine, although there were still those who chose to fit the tank behind the engine.

Virtually all early machines were started by pedalling, and were fitted with standard cycle-type pedals for this purpose. This tended to dictate the frame geometry and ergonomics and, for this reason – plus the fact that most pioneering motorcycle manufacturers had graduated from pedal cycles – early machines strongly resemble pedal cycles. Inertia kick starters were quick to appear and pedals had disappeared completely by around 1915. Indian tried to introduce electric start before World War I but the system was unreliable and almost bankrupted the company.

ABOVE: **Although it dates from the inter-war years, this Harley-Davidson clearly shows the standardized motorcycle layout which quickly emerged.** LEFT: **As with this early Triumph, some manufacturers continued to use belt drive even after the virtues of the roller chain had been well proven.**

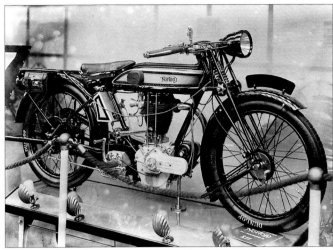

Electric start became the norm in the 1970s and 1980s as Japanese imports stormed the world markets.

Some early pioneers used a two- or even three-speed epicyclic gearbox, placing this in the rear hub, following the style of the pedal cycle; this also allowed the clutch to be fitted in the hub. Pioneered by Triumph on their 500cc Model H, the most logical position for the gearbox was behind the engine, with the clutch placed between the engine and gearbox, and this was quickly adopted by all manufacturers. So-called unitary construction techniques subsequently incorporated the gearbox into the crankcase casting.

While the use of a rear brake was almost universal, it was some time before all manufacturers also fitted brakes for the front wheel, and many riders still believed that the use of a front brake was dangerous. Rim brakes gave way to drum brakes, and then to the universal adoption of disc brakes; similarly, mechanical

operation by rod or cable eventually yielded to hydraulics, meaning that it was no longer necessary to provide huge brake levers in order to get sufficient leverage to stop a heavy machine.

The standard layout described had become pretty much universal on all motorcycles by the outbreak of World War I but, curiously, it was decades before there was any agreement on where the brake, clutch and gear-change controls should be placed. Specifically, there were differences between machines produced in Europe and the USA, and this must have led to more than a few accidents or near-misses as riders rode on unfamiliar machines during the two wars. Harley-Davidson, for example, used a left-hand throttle and hand gear-change on the war-time WLA, and continued to offer a hand gear-change right up to 1972/73. These days, only motor scooters, with their rear engines and lack of foot controls, seem to vary from this standard layout.

ABOVE: **Although broadly conforming to the norm, this early Norton has the magneto carried ahead of the frame down-tube, a position favoured by more than one British manufacturer.** ABOVE LEFT: **The distinctive gear change lever on the Harley-Davidson was always mounted on the left-hand side of the fuel tank.** LEFT: **The British Matchless G3L of 1941 was one of the first military motorcycles to adopt telescopic front forks.**

Military Motorcycles from World War I to 1939

The development of the military motorcycle has followed the same path as the civilian machines. Little more than pedal bicycles with a motor, early motorcycles had either a V-belt or chain to transmit power to the rear wheel. Frequently, the pedals remained in place, providing a means of starting the engine and assisting the power unit to drag machine and rider up an incline.

World War I brought an enormous upsurge in the use of motorcycles in Europe and the United States. Around this time, motorcycles started to enter military service, replacing mounted despatch riders and providing a means of mechanizing machine-gun and stretcher units.

This chapter covers the history of the military motorcycle from World War I to 1939, highlighting the varied roles motorcycles have played, as well as how the vehicles have evolved over time. Special topics include the expansion of military usage, civilian motorcycles going to war, horse power giving way to horsepower, specialist roles for the motorcycle, motorcycle stretcher bearers, the Great Depression and tracked motorcycles.

LEFT: **Exhaustion enables a man to sleep anywhere. This World War II Canadian despatch rider has managed to use his Norton 16H as a makeshift bunk.**

Expanding military usage

During the opening years of the 20th century, motorcycles began to improve significantly in reliability and, as the design of the machines also started to settle down, the number of motorcycle manufacturers expanded rapidly. The military started to take an interest in these new machines and the manufacturers began to vie with one another for military contracts. By 1905 it

was obvious that there was a real role for the military motorcycle and, in Britain, companies such as Scott, Triumph and BSA had started to supply motorcycles to the Army, with purchases often being under the control of individual commanding officers. In Germany, it was a similar story, where the first German military motorcycles had entered service as early as 1901.

Among civilians, the popularity of the motorcycle was progressing in leaps and bounds. By 1913, there were 100,000 motorcycles registered in Britain, and by 1914, many of the major European and American manufacturers had already been established – Triumph, BSA, AJS, Norton, Indian, Harley-Davidson, Puch, Peugeot and NSU were in business before 1914, and all would go on to have a major influence on the industry over the next 50 years. All of these companies would also become major suppliers to the world's armed forces.

When World War I broke out in 1914, the demand for motorcycles took another unprecedented leap forward. Thousands of civilian machines were requisitioned and pressed into service alongside those that had been supplied direct to the military. However, while the war may have been a catalyst for production, it did little for innovation. The armed forces may have purchased thousands of motorcycles but they tended to favour reliability over innovation, effectively forcing the manufacturers to be conservative. At the same time, the civilian market shrank and many small companies did not make it through the war years.

By the end of the war, the German *Reichswehr* had an inventory of 5,400 motorcycles, mostly civilian types that had received little more militarization than a coat of matt paint and

ABOVE: **Germany was quick to see the advantages of the motorcycle in military terms and, by 1914, had almost 5,400 motorcycles available.** LEFT: **Early motorcycles were not necessarily reliable, as this Highlander would certainly attest.**

LEFT: **The 2.75hp machine produced by the British manufacturer Douglas was widely adopted by the British Army, with more than 13,000 in service by 1918. Douglas retained the V-belt drive and exposed flywheel into the post-war years.**
BELOW LEFT: **The water-cooled Scott 3.25hp was used by the British Army as a machine-gun carrier. The machines operated in threes, one with a tripod-mounted gun, one with just the tripod, and one carrying parts and/or personnel.**

a pillion seat. But this number paled into insignificance against the British Army's 1918 total of 48,000 machines from more than 50 different manufacturers – a fact which can hardly have helped the problems of maintaining adequate stocks of spare parts.

France had been one of the first nations to embrace mechanization of its army and, although the nation's army did not employ large numbers of motorcycles during World War I, companies such as René Gillet, Peugeot, Griffon and Terrot had started supplying military motorcycles from the

turn of the century. In Belgium, the armaments company FN produced their first motorcycles in 1902, and their products were supplied to a number of the Western Allies during the conflict, including Australia.

The US Army was slower to embrace the new developments and did not start buying motorcycles until about 1913. Nevertheless, something like 15,000 Harley-Davidsons and 18,000 (Hendee) Indians were supplied during World War I, with other machines coming from Excelsior and Cleveland, as well as from British manufacturers such as Rover and Triumph.

Italy started to procure military motorcycles in 1914, and the nation had something like 6,500 machines in service by the time the conflict came to an end.

By 1918, all of the major combatants had acquired large stocks of motorcycles and, at the end of the conflict, thousands of surplus motorcycles were put up for sale across Europe and America, with ex-servicemen among the eager buyers. Those manufacturers who were still in business returned to producing purely civilian machines, some with little more than modified pre-war models. But, for many, the war had been invaluable in improving the breed and the new machines were considerably more reliable than their pre-war counterparts.

The motorcycle had finally come of age and technological progress in the post-war period was rapid, with features such as chain drive, electric lighting, and front and rear brakes becoming the norm. New manufacturers would continue to spring up over the coming decades and many of the early pioneers were seen to fail, but this was a period of exciting technological progress, with specialized heavyweight military machines starting to appear in the decade before World War II.

ABOVE: **Typical of civilian motorcycles of the period, the Triumph Model H, which was nicknamed "Trusty" for its reliability, was widely used by the British Army.**

Civilian motorcycles go to war

The earliest military motorcycles were basic civilian machines. Most armies had not started to evolve any motor vehicle policy and there was little attempt made at standardization. With the outbreak of World War I, it was soon apparent that there was a shortage of motorcycles and many were requisitioned. Others entered service and remained privately owned, effectively "loaned" to the army by their civilian volunteer riders. Militarization, such as it was, generally consisted of little more than fitting leather panniers and a rear rack, and painting the machine with the typical overall matt grey or green finish that was supposed to hide its outline from the all-seeing field glasses of the enemy.

At the time it must have seemed that issues such as reliability and performance were largely a matter of chance and, until the outbreak of World War I, the military usage of motorcycles was such that there had been little opportunity for any specialized requirements to emerge. Civilian motorcycles were widely available and it should

ABOVE: **Aside from the inevitable, although not necessarily universal, coat of matt green paint, early military motorcycles were rarely different to their civilian counterparts.**
RIGHT: **Posing in front of the Austin armoured cars that were supplied to the Imperial Army during World War I, these Russian soldiers are equipped with two bicycles and three civilian motorcycles of indeterminate origin.**

be no surprise that it was these which the world's armies started to buy from around the turn of the century. However, when World War I led to huge increases in the numbers of motorcycles required, the sheer diversity of types which entered in service began to present something of a logistical nightmare that was never really resolved.

In Britain, the Government banned the sale of motorcycles to civilians in 1916, diverting many of those who had been making motorcycles to the production of other war supplies. But this had no effect on the types of machine available and orders continued to be placed with the remaining manufacturers for the duration of the conflict for what were essentially civilian machines. By 1918, some 48,000 motorcycles remained in service with the British Army, drawn from a list of manufacturers that reads like a roll-call of the early industry: Ariel, BSA, Clyno, Douglas, James, Norton, Rover, Rudge, Scott, Sunbeam, Triumph, and others now long-forgotten. However, the majority of the machines came from just two manufacturers. Triumph supplied 30,000 examples of the 550cc Model H – known as the "Trusty" – while Douglas provided 25,000 examples of their 348cc Model V. Both had started life as civilian machines. The

ABOVE: **Although its origins were civilian, the Douglas 2.75hp twin-cylinder solo machine was the closest thing to a standardized military motorcycle in the British Army, second only to the Triumph Model H in numbers. A larger 4hp model was used for sidecar duties.**

Douglas was a pre-war design, with a somewhat antiquated V-belt drive and two-speed gearbox, while the more modern Triumph had been launched in 1915.

The German and Austrian armies used rather less motorcycles than Britain but, having realized the importance of reliability, had early on decided to choose only those machines which could be shown to be capable of withstanding the rigours of a service life. As early as 1899, the German Imperial Army had established the *Inspektion de Verkehrstrüppen* to test prototype military vehicles, including motorcycles. The products of NSU – known at the time as Neckarsulm – and Triumph were among the first motorcycles to be considered suitable for military use. NSU supplied three different militarized civilian models, the lightweight 190cc Pony, and two types of V-twin, a 499cc machine rated at 3.5hp, and a big 995cc model rated at 7–9hp, while Triumph (TWN) supplied their 489cc JAP-engined 4.25hp machine. Puch and Wanderer were also important suppliers, and many civilian machines, of various makes, were also requisitioned.

The US Army deployed domestic motorcycles from Hendee (Indian), Harley-Davidson, Excelsior and Cleveland, alongside requisitioned machines and the products of a number of the British motorcycle factories.

It was not until the post-World War I years that the specialized military motorcycle started to emerge.

LEFT: **Harley-Davidson started supplying motorcycles to the US Army in 1916. Photographed in France in 1919, this essentially civilian V-twin Model J is typical of the machines produced by the company during World War I.**

Horse power gives way to horsepower

At the turn of the last century, the motorcycle was still in its infancy and many of the machines being produced were primitive, unreliable and difficult to ride. And yet by 1914, when the opposing armies of Britain and Germany faced each other across the flat lands that lay between France and Belgium, motorcycles had become relatively commonplace. Many soldiers had ridden such machines in civilian life and it must have seemed perfectly logical that the motorcycle would begin to replace the horse in the military world in the same way that it been replacing the horse elsewhere. While the motorcycle could not pull a heavy field piece, replace a cavalry mount or transport large numbers of men and supplies, the inherent flexibility and mobility of the machine allowed it to be adopted for a variety of military roles.

When World War I broke out, it had been just 15 years since Vickers & Maxim Limited had demonstrated a single-cylinder motor quadricycle adapted to carry a crew of two and an air-cooled Maxim machine-gun to the British War Office. None was purchased, but conventional military motorcycles followed soon after. The German Army's first military motorcycles were purchased in 1904 and the US government bought Indian Powerplus machines as early as 1913. By 1916, the first Harley-Davidsons were being used to pursue Francisco "Pancho" Villa – into Mexico, where legend has it that Villa's men were mounted on Indian motorcycles. However, even at this stage, not everyone believed that the motorcycle was necessarily the way forward.

ABOVE: **An early civilian specification Triumph Model H, in front of armoured cars of the Royal Naval Air Service.** BELOW: **The single-cylinder BSA Model H was typical of the solo machines used during World War I; the British Army had more than 500 in service by the end of the conflict.**

Looking back, many now consider World War I to be the first mechanized conflict, but in the early years, the opposing sides were still continuing to rely on mounted despatch riders and runners to convey messages. However,

ABOVE: **Sidecars were frequently seen as a means of providing transportation for officers in the field.** LEFT: **BSA began motorcycle production in 1911 and their belt-drive Model H, dating from 1914, was widely supplied to the Allies during World War I.**

as the conflict wore on, the ground conditions deteriorated to such a point that the motorcycle appeared to offer the most effective means of transporting messages. The British Signals Corps' despatch riders adopted motorcycles in place of horses, sometimes getting the best of both worlds by attaching baskets for carrier pigeons to the machines, bringing the pigeons closer to the front to reduce the transit time for the message.

Frequently, motorcycles were the only vehicles able to negotiate the terrible conditions, and sidecar outfits were adapted to provide a means of evacuating the wounded from the trenches to the casualty clearing stations. A sidecar outfit also provided a flexible form of transport, allowing equipment and ammunition to be brought up to the front line across ground which heavier transport was unable to negotiate.

The motorcycle also provided a means of mobilizing machine-guns and both sides experimented with machine-gun sidecars, usually with some sort of simple armoured screen for the gunner. It must have been immediately obvious that there was no prospect of firing accurately on the move but at least the motorcycle allowed the gunner to move rapidly from one location to another using the technique that is now called "shoot and scoot".

By the end of the war, it was obvious that there had been a change. The military motorcycle became the

preferred choice over the horse or mule for the transport of personnel and light supplies, as well as providing the perfect mount for couriers and despatch riders.

ABOVE: **This motorcycle is a Harley-Davidson under control of the American Red Cross, but the sidecars are on the left, suggesting that the machine is to be used in Britain.**

23

War production

In 1914, there were 200 motorcycle manufacturers in Britain and, for the first years of the war, business continued much as before – if they were lucky, some of them received the bonus of some nice big military contracts. Then, in late 1916, the British Government banned the sale of motorcycles to civilians, an act which helped those manufacturers whose products were approved but pushed many companies into bankruptcy.

Like much of the British engineering sector, the unlucky motorcycle manufacturers were forced to turn to other defence work. A few were allowed to continue to produce motorcycles which were considered useful to the military alongside other government work. For example, BSA and Royal Enfield resumed the mass production of guns and parts for guns, although both were also allowed to continue to manufacture motorcycles. For BSA, this led to considerable expansion and, although there was no further land available at the company's Small Heath works, the demand for motorcycles from Britain, France and Russia was such that a new production facility was constructed at Redditch, which placed the company in a very strong position when the war was over.

At Triumph's nearby Coventry factory, some 30,000 examples of the chain-drive Model H were supplied to the Allied forces – 20,000 of which went to the British Army. Demand for the machine was such that Triumph profited considerably from the war and it is interesting to note that at the end of the war, Colonel Claude Vivian Holbrook who had been responsible for motorcycle procurement for the War Office joined Triumph as general manager.

Douglas produced 25,000 machines during the war years, putting them just behind Triumph as the second-largest manufacturer, and Phelon & Moore – later trading as Panther –

were in third place with something like 3,500 machines produced, their 3.5hp machine having become the standard mount for the Royal Flying Corps.

Alongside the manufacture of a single military model, Matchless turned to the production of aircraft parts. Sunbeam turned out radiators for motor vehicles and aircraft as well as motorcycles, many of which went to the French. Rudge was forced to discontinue the production of motorcycles in 1916 and concentrate on munitions and aircraft wheels. Ariel, James, Norton and Rover continued to supply motorcycles, many of

ABOVE: **To accommodate the demand for all of the company's products, BSA built a new factory at Redditch, England, which placed the company in a very strong position after the war.** RIGHT: **New BSA motorcycles awaiting despatch to France.**

LEFT: **Photographed in BSA's new Redditch facility, the overhead line-shafting and belt-drive machinery arranged in serried ranks is typical of machine shops of the period. The lack of guarding is surprising to modern eyes.** BELOW: **Employee welfare became increasingly important during the war years and companies such as BSA started to provide medical, canteen and social facilities. Women also began to become increasingly important in the workplace.**

which were destined for Russia but, unable to complete the deliveries because of the 1917 Revolution, the machines remained stockpiled at the ports.

For other companies, things were different and while some were able to resume motorcycle manufacture in 1919, others disappeared.

In Germany, NSU concentrated on the manufacture of munitions but still found time to produce the majority of the motorcycles used by the Imperial German Army, and their 3.5hp machine became the most widely used German military motorcycle. The largest Austrian company, Puch, produced only small numbers of machines between 1914 and 1918 but went on to become a major motorcycle supplier in the immediate post-war years.

In a reverse of the situation in Europe, Harley-Davidson production was initially affected by the war in Europe to the extent that certain imported components became unavailable and the cost of iron and steel, rubber and other raw materials rose in response to increased demand – the consequent increase in the price of their products affected sales adversely. The US Army began buying military motorcycles in 1916, and Indian devoted almost their entire production facility to the war effort, choosing deliberately to stop selling to civilians. While Indian offered 20,000 machines to the US Government in 1916, with a similar figure for 1917, Harley supplied just 7,000 in each of the two years. In 1918, Harley started to construct a new factory and when the war was over, was in a strong position to take Indian's number one sales spot.

By the time the war was over, the US motorcycle industry had supplied almost 60,000 motorcycles to the war effort, 41,000 of which came from Indian.

By 1918, military contracts had been cancelled or scaled down but, development had been put on hold during the conflict, and many British and European motorcycle manufacturers were hardly in a position to put new models on to a market that would soon be awash with surplus machines. It was to be some years before the industry recovered.

25

Dressing the part

During the first two years of World War I, more than three million men volunteered to serve in the British Armed Forces. Many of the motorcycle despatch riders who signed up to the Signals Corps during this period were what these days we would term enthusiasts, men who had enjoyed motorcycling during the pre-war years and who joined up willingly in the belief that they would be able to serve their country while also riding a motorbike at the same time. These men required no training, but the rates of attrition on the Western Front meant that this situation could not continue.

In 1916, Britain introduced conscription and many of the men who followed had little idea of how to ride a motorcycle and needed training in how to handle their machines, how to find their way and how to undertake simple maintenance. Military training centres were established for this purpose but the combination of relatively untrained riders and fragile machines was not a good one.

ABOVE: **Crash helmets did not exist during World War I. This man, balancing a pigeon basket on his sidecar, is using his steel helmet as protection.** ABOVE LEFT: **A British officer attired in leather boots, pith helmet and a cartridge bandolier.**

While it is easy to relate to the need for training – and at the same time to underestimate the importance of the standardization in the layout of the motorcycle's controls which had yet to take place – it is just as easy to underestimate the hardships which these early riders endured. Dirt roads kicked up clouds of filthy dust during the summer and turned to seas of mud in the winter. The widespread use of sharp stone road dressings led to frequent punctures, while wet or icy cobbles or granite setts, such as were common in France and Belgium, presented their own set of hazards.

Riding a motorcycle was a dirty business. The total-loss lubrication systems that were the order of the day meant that the machine was inevitably covered in a film of oil and dust that was guaranteed to make any clothing filthy. Primitive suspension systems, combined with high-pressure tyres gave a hard bumpy ride which shook the machines apart and necessitated frequent rest stops during which the rider would have to check that his machine was fit to continue. It was not uncommon for the rider to be expected to mend a puncture by the roadside, or to refit a drive chain or belt, or clean a spark plug fouled by dirty fuel.

But, perhaps most important, purpose-designed protective clothing was non existent. In cold weather the early motorcyclist would dress in layers of thick clothing, his hands would be encased in stiff gloves and, for his feet, there was nothing more than horse-riding or working boots.

LEFT: **World War I re-enactors dress in the correct uniform of the day. Riding breeches and boots are not really the thing for riding motorcycles.**

LEFT: **It is hard to imagine that the typical peaked cap would remain in place at any speed.** ABOVE: **US infantrymen wearing the regulation puttees and steel helmets; the bag on the man's chest almost certainly contains a gas mask.**

rags under their clothing to provide an extra layer of insulation; but it must have been desperately uncomfortable.

Although the Germans had a crude protective hat for motorcyclists, and the French seemed keen on riding a motorcycle wearing the standard military protective steel helmet, proper crash helmets did not exist and it is equally common to see photographs of men riding these early machines with their head protected only by a cloth cap or peaked military hat. Hinged glass flying goggles were generally used to keep dust, and the ever-present flies of the Western Front, out of the eyes.

In wet weather, oilskins or a cape might be worn in an attempt to keep dry. Spare parts and tools were often carried in a backpack and spare inner tubes could be worn around the shoulders or wrapped around the handlebars.

But hardship breeds camaraderie and these early despatch riders considered themselves to be a very special breed, united by their own particular brand of hell and a breed that was apart from the common foot soldier.

Military despatch riders were required to ride in uniform, and a military greatcoat, flapping in the wind, was not exactly the best way to keep warm and dry. The British Army issued motorcyclists with high boots or leather gaiters to replace the standard puttees, and a special mackintosh for winter use, but nevertheless, many men resorted to stuffing newspaper or

LEFT: **In 1933, the German Army developed a special motorcyclist's coat – the *Kradmantel*. It remained in widespread use until the end of World War II.** BELOW: **British despatch riders of World War II wearing the regulation uniform for the role.**

27

Specialist roles for the motorcycle

The majority of the motorcycles deployed by the Allies and the Central Powers in World War I were of civilian origin. In the case of despatch riders and messengers these motorcycles were used in the same way that they would have been used in civvy street, but there also evolved specialized roles which had no civilian equivalent.

The combat role is a good case in point. Back in those early days there must have been a tendency to view the motorcycle and rider as a mechanized cavalryman and this suggested that the motorcycle could be assigned a front-line role. Conversely, the role of evacuating the wounded, was almost certainly forced on to the motorcycle by virtue of the condition of the ground around the front line, where it was simply impossible to make any progress in a conventional motor ambulance.

Motorcycle-mounted machine-guns

The machine-gun was the "weapon of mass destruction" of the late 19th and early 20th centuries. The Maxim gun was the first machine-gun to use the recoil energy to eject each spent cartridge and insert the next, making it far more efficient than previous hand-cranked multi-barrel weapons. It was first used by Britain's colonial forces in the First Matabele War (1893–94) where, in one engagement, 50 soldiers are said to have fought off 5,000 warriors with just four Maxim guns. With a high rate of cyclical fire, a single machine-gun could cover a broad sweep of territory, indiscriminately cutting down any soldier foolish enough to venture into the field of fire and, by the first year of World War I, both sides were deploying improved machine-guns with terrifying rates of fire.

ABOVE: **A Harley-Davidson Model FUS fitted with a special ammunition sidecar during World War I. Unusually, the rider is a military policeman.**

The Imperial German Army had integrated the weapon fully into its organization structure and in the first year of the war, had something like 12,000 machine-guns; by 1916, motorcycles were attached to all machine-gun sections. Although the standard German Maxim-derived gun weighed 19kg/43lb and was too heavy to be manhandled or used by an individual, it was sufficiently compact to mount on a motorcycle sidecar, sometimes with a simple armoured shield, and required only three men to form an efficient crew. Two or three mobile machine-gun teams could quickly move from one location to another, carrying guns, crews, ammunition and spares on their motorcycles. The Germans even mounted machine-guns on solo motorcycles.

In Britain, too, the War Department had been thinking of mounting machine-guns on sidecars since the turn of the century, and in the USA, Harley-Davidson supplied machine-gun sidecars from 1916.

During World War I, British machine-gun motorcycles operated in teams of three, in support of infantry advances or attacking isolated enemy positions. Although the gun was mounted in such a way that it could be fired on the move, it must have become obvious almost immediately that this was a non-starter. Trying to control a machine-gun from a bucking sidecar would, in many cases, have presented what these days we would describe as a "friendly fire" incident, with equal hazards experienced by both sides. However, one contemporary popular source described

ABOVE: **Although, as seen below, there were specialist pigeon loft sidecars, these men have strapped the pigeon basket to their backs and are riding solo machines.**
LEFT: **A special driven sidecar was developed for the Belgian Army and was used with FN, Gillet-Herstal and Sarolea motorcycles.**

the result as an "efficient little engine of war, large numbers of which are used on active service (where) they are in great demand for scouting and reconnoitring purposes where rapidity of movement is so essential".

Despite their shortcomings, both sides persevered with motorcycle-mounted machine-guns to the end of the conflict.

Motorcycle stretcher bearers

During the five years of total warfare, the toll of dead and wounded was on a scale that hitherto would have been unbelievable. The Allies lost more than 5 million men in action, with a further 12.88 million wounded; the armies of the Central Powers lost more than 3.38 million men, with 9 million wounded.

On the Allied side, this represents an injury rate of 8,241 men a day and the task of evacuating these men from the front line, assessing their injuries and assigning them for further

treatment was formidable. While there was often no alternative to carrying the wounded from the trenches to a relatively safe rear area, equally, the motorcycle was often the only practicable means of getting the man to the next link in the chain which might eventually see him repatriated to the UK.

All of the combatants used motorcycles in this role, sometimes, as in the case of the British Sunbeam, using a purpose-made sidecar, at other times simply making do with strapping the stretcher to the sidecar chassis.

Other roles

During the early days, motorcycle sidecar outfits were also used to carry pigeon lofts and baskets and, when pigeons gave way to up-to-date wireless equipment. Sidecars were also used to accommodate the relatively bulky accumulators, chargers, aerial masts, and transmitters and receivers.

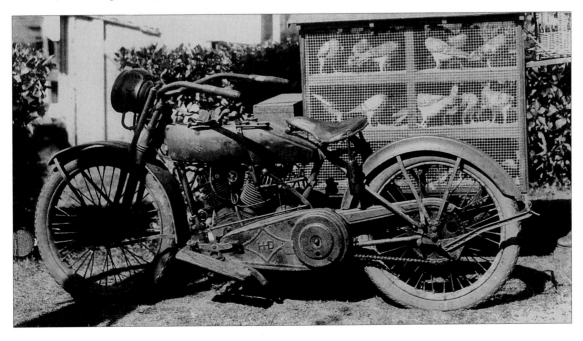

LEFT: **Photographed in June 1930, this Harley-Davidson outfit has been equipped with a pigeon loft sidecar. Pigeons were still used for communication into World War II.**

Motorcycle stretcher bearers

As well as lending itself to mounting a machine-gun, during World War I, the relative mobility of the motorcycle across the cratered ground of the ebbing and flowing front line led to the machines being used for other roles. Most significant of these was the use of the sidecar as a stretcher carrier.

In all conflicts it had been the practice of the Royal Army Medical Corps (RAMC) to establish a chain of medical establishments stretching from the front-line positions back to hospitals in the United Kingdom or, for example, India. The first step involved regimental stretcher bearers – during World War I these were not RAMC men but were often regimental bandsmen who had received some rudimentary first aid training – taking the wounded man to a Regimental Aid Post (RAP), a small, often temporary position near the front line where some treatment could be delivered. From here, RAMC Field Ambulance stretcher bearers would collect those wounded that required further treatment and deliver them to the Field Ambulance Advanced Dressing Stations (ADS), if further evacuation were needed, the casualty would be moved to a Clearing Hospital, later called a Casualty Clearing Station, and then, by rail and ship back to Britain.

At first, horse ambulances, and then motor ambulances, were employed to move the wounded from the Aid Posts to the Dressing Stations but, in the absence of good roads, the motorcycle sidecar provided an excellent, if somewhat uncomfortable, alternative. If the evacuation was taking place close to the front, the machines were driven by men but,

ABOVE: **During World War I Sunbeam produced a special softly sprung sidecar for the medical evacuation role.** BELOW: **Motorcycles were widely used as stretcher carriers but, as this open double-decker shows, not every injured man had the benefit of even the most basic weather protection.**

in the relative safety of the behind-the-lines areas, it was not uncommon for the riders to be women volunteers – and more than a few lost their lives when shelling went astray.

These were not sophisticated machines and any ride for a wounded man must have involved considerable discomfort. In its crudest form, the ambulance consisted of little more than a stretcher strapped across the sidecar

LEFT: **Clearly the man's injuries are not life threatening and he is almost certainly on his way from the front-line Dressing Station to a medical facility somewhere behind the lines. The sidecar offers very little protection but at least his feet are covered and one must hope that he is strapped in.**

chassis, with a blanket or canvas cover used to keep the injured man warm. Even the better ambulances included no more than a folding cover to protect the occupant from the elements. Weight was always an issue in developing more comfortable alternatives and although the British company Watsonian started building completely covered sidecar ambulances with special springs in 1916, and both Harley-Davidson and the US-based Flxible Sidecar Company built purpose-made ambulance sidecars for the US Army, the motorcycle ambulance was at best a necessary evil. Similar equipment was deployed by the French, German and Belgian armies.

The practice remained widespread during World War I and the US Army certainly continued to equip its medical service with motorcycle sidecars during the 1920s but the more mobile nature of the conflict during World War II, and the use of Jeep stretcher-bearers and other four-wheel drive vehicles, had rendered the motorcycle stretcher bearer almost, but not quite obsolete by 1940. The US Army was using a scooter sidecar combination, equipped with an almost coffin like lidded rectangular box, to move patients around the site of an Army hospital in Northern Ireland in 1943. The inclusion of emergency lights suggest that it was used to get casualties from incoming medevac flights into the emergency rooms.

LEFT: **Motorcycles were still being used for medical evacuation during World War II but almost certainly only during airborne operations when conventional ambulances were not available. The two-wheeled stretcher carrier would not normally have been towed – even behind a four-wheeled vehicle.**

Armoured and machine-gun motorcycles

In 1899 Frederick R. Simms designed the "motor scout" for Vickers, Son & Maxim. It was little more than a motorized quadricycle on which was mounted a water-cooled Maxim machine-gun but it seemed to offer mobility for the machine-gun. Contemporary photographs show an incongruously bowler-hatted rider crouched behind a small armoured screen and, while there was almost certainly never any question of firing on the move, the machine would have permitted motorcycle troops to move with relative speed from one firing point to another, as well as allowing multiple machine-guns to act in concert, laying down interlocking fields of fire.

The machine was demonstrated to the War Office, but no decisions were made regarding series production.

However, while the "motor scout" might not have been quite the right machine for the job, the notion of mounting a machine-gun behind a small armoured screen on a motorcycle was clearly an idea whose time had come. Just months into World War I, British Army Order 480, dated November 12, 1914, approved the creation of Motor Machine Gun (MMG) batteries, attached to the Royal Field Artillery. By September 1915, there were 18 MMG battalions in France, mounted for the most part on Clyno and Scott motorcycles – although Matchless, Premier, Zenith and Enfield machines were also used – carrying a water-cooled Vickers machine-gun on a special sidecar. There was no protection for the rider but the gunner was provided with a small armoured screen. The machines were operated in threes, one equipped with a gun, one carrying a spare tripod position, and a third with ammunition and spares.

Collectively, these units were known as the Motor Machine Gun Service (MMGS) and special efforts were made to enlist men known to be interested in motorcycling – the Coventry office of the enthusiasts' magazine *Motor Cycle* was even designated as a recruiting office. However, it soon became obvious that to be fully effective, machine-guns needed to be used in larger units and, in October 1915, the MMGS was incorporated into the newly formed Machine Gun Corps (MGC) which had infantry, cavalry and motor branches. Each motor battery of the MGC included 18 sidecar combinations, carrying

ABOVE: **Mounting a water-cooled Vickers machine-gun behind an armoured shield, the British Clyno/Vickers outfit was widely used by the Machine Gun Corps. The gun could also be dismounted and used on its tripod from a ground position.**
RIGHT: **By September 1915, there were 18 Motor Machine Gun Battalions in France, mounted for the most part on Clyno (as shown) and Scott motorcycles – although Matchless, Premier, Zenith and Enfield motorcycles were also used.**

six Vickers machine-guns with ammunition and spare equipment; eight motorcycles without sidecars; two or three wagons or cars; and a sidecar combination for the commanding officer.

This approach was not unique to the British Army and in 1915 the *Reichswehr* also started to mount rear-facing machine-guns on to the sidecars of NSU 7hp motorcycles; once again, the gunner had a small armoured screen which gave a measure of protection. And in the USA, during 1916, Harley-Davidson supplied the US Army with a number of sidecar-equipped Model J outfits, which allowed tripod-mounting of a machine-gun behind a folding armoured shield; unlike the British and German machines, there was a seat for the gunner, and a small degree of armoured protection was provided for the rider in the form of leg shields. Excelsior machines were similarly used, equipped with the FIxible sidecar.

The end of World War I did not quite spell the end of the road for the armoured motorcycle and throughout the 1920s and 1930s, various experiments were carried out in an attempt to provide cheap, mobile armoured vehicles for snipers.

For example, in 1932, a Harley-Davidson VSC/LC sidecar outfit was supplied to the Swedish company Landsverk for conversion to an armoured machine-gun mount for the Danish Army. This time, both gunner and rider were enclosed by an armoured hull; the gunner faced to the rear and fired a machine-gun through an armoured screen, or dismounted to use the gun from in front of the machine in the anti-aircraft role. The weight can have done little for the machine's performance and the experiment, known as the Landsverk 210, was abandoned.

ABOVE: **The water-cooled Vickers was not the only gun mounted on a motorcycle; this photograph shows a drum-fed Lewis machine-gun.**

The Italian Army specified the Moto-Guzzi GT17, also dating from 1932, with forward-facing armoured protection for the rider and a machine-gun mount and, although it was not equipped with a gun, in one of its incarnations, Mercier's curious half-tracked motorcycle of 1936 was provided with a curved armoured screen to protect the rider. The following year, Venezuela and Argentina both purchased a number of Belgian FN M86 combination outfits that were fitted with armoured screens and sidecars, and the Danish Army also deployed Nimbus sidecar machines which were equipped with Madsen machine-guns on a special military sidecar.

Eventually it was realized that the motorcycle's strengths lay elsewhere and, the only use of armoured machines during World War II seems to have been the 1942 Moto-Guzzi *Triace*, examples of which mounted a rear-facing heavy machine-gun behind an armoured shield.

ABOVE: **By the end of World War I, the British Army had almost 1,800 Clynos in service, many of which were used as machine-gun carriers.** LEFT: **The gun was rarely fired from the sidecar but, of course, the motorcycle provided excellent mobility, allowing the crew to adopt the modern "shoot and scoot" tactic.**

Peacetime returns

In 1918, all outstanding British and US military motorcycle contracts were cancelled as, of course, were those in Germany and Austria. However, there is little doubt that the military use of motorcycles during World War I had helped to further the motorcycle industry, both in the UK and in the USA. Innovation may have taken a back seat, but the machines became more reliable, and the manufacturers learned how to increase productivity to meet the military demands for their products – BSA, for example, had opened a huge new four-storey factory in 1915 to cope with the Army's demands.

Many returning soldiers had been exposed to motorcycles for the first time during their military service and became potential customers when peace returned. At the same time, the real increases in productivity allowed post-war civilian prices to be lowered.

Civilian production in post-war Britain resumed almost immediately, although the strike in Glasgow during 1919 supporting a reduced 40-hour working week in many industries, including iron and steel, had a serious effect on production, affecting most manufacturers. However, there was considerable pent-up consumer demand and, in 1919, the first national exhibition of motorcycles was held at Olympia in London, with 112 manufacturers showing their products, and with more than one appearing for the first time. The number of motorcycle manufacturers in Britain continued to grow steadily and, in the three years following the end of the war, about 100 new manufacturers joined the industry. The machines themselves became increasingly sophisticated and, by 1920, there were more than a quarter of a million motorcycles registered in Britain. Motorcycle production hit an all-time high in Britain in 1929, when some 147,000 machines were produced.

Despite the burgeoning civilian market, the British Army was happy to continue to operate surplus machines from the war years. In fact, it was to be a further decade before the British

TOP: **The US Army's motorcycle dump in France, 1918. The machines are awaiting disposal.** ABOVE: **There is more than one military use for a motorcycle.**

Army took further significant interest in acquiring, or even testing, new motorcycles.

In the USA the story was somewhat different perhaps due, in part, to competition from Henry Ford's Model T which had appeared in 1908 and which was selling half a million units a year by 1915. There had been 200 US-based motorcycle manufacturers when the US Expeditionary Force left for Europe in 1917 but, within two years of the end of the war, this number had been reduced to less than 40. The largest of these were Excelsior, Harley-Davidson and Indian, all of which had invested heavily in their production facilities during 1917 and 1918. However, Indian had relied too heavily on military contracts and, when these came to an end, the company was unable to fund the recovery of its civilian markets. Harley-Davidson was in considerably better shape, having

LEFT: **Although the belt-drive machines are decidedly antique in appearance, these Belgian motorcyclists date from the immediate post-war years.**

never really abandoned civilian production, and sales during the 1919 model year – the first with no military contracts – totalled around 24,000. In 1918, Harley-Davidson had also borrowed $3 million and started the construction of a new manufacturing facility and, although Excelsior managed to sell 100,000 machines during 1919, Harley-Davidson had become the largest motorcycle manufacturer in the world by 1920. By the end of the decade, the big three US motorcycle companies comprised the entire US motorcycle industry.

Elsewhere in Europe, it was to be a decade or so before new manufacturers started to enter the industry but it is certainly worth recording that 1919 was the year that BMW started to look at the motorcycle industry. Forbidden by the Treaty of Versailles to manufacture aircraft, BMW's head designer Max Fritz, considered producing motorcycle and motorcar engines to sustain the company. It took him just four weeks to complete the drawings for the now-famous "Boxer" engine and a production example was installed in a motorcycle just two years later, albeit not under the BMW name.

ABOVE: **The machine is an Indian of the early 1920s, and the riders are clearly in uniform, but the reason for the front-wheel disc is not known. Note the semi-elliptical multi-leaf suspension on the front forks.**
RIGHT: **The German Army of the inter-war years purchased thousands of motorcycles, with dozens of different, mostly civilian style, models. There was a total of one million such machines in military service by 1937.**

35

The Great Depression

While the 1920s were a time of increasing civilian sales, the Great Depression of the early 1930s told a different story altogether. Britain and the USA were the worst affected, with too many companies chasing too few customers, but the global nature of the Depression meant that export sales were hit equally hard. The British government introduced a tax on large engines, forcing domestic manufacturers to concentrate on small and inexpensive models and by 1932–33, as conditions started to improve, many manufacturers had closed their doors for good. By the end of the Depression in the USA, the only manufacturers to survive were Harley-Davidson and Indian, Excelsior having finally called in the receivers in 1931. However, during this period the design of motorcycle continued to improve and evolve even if military and civilian sales were slow.

The British Army had made few new purchases since 1918 but, by the end of the 1920s, those World War I machines which remained in service were becoming outdated and the War Office started to draw up a set of requirements for the perfect military motorcycle. The newly established Mechanical Warfare Experimental Establishment (MWEE) was set the task of examining every motorcycle available at the time. During 1929, examples of 350cc production machines were purchased from seven British manufacturers – AJS, BSA, Douglas, Francis Barnett, Matchless, New Hudson and OEC – with the notion that they would be put through a series

ABOVE: **For many manufacturers, the 1930s was a time of dwindling sales and many of the smaller companies, particularly those who persevered with labour-intensive construction methods, failed to survive.**

RIGHT: **This method of assembling motorcycles on static benches was not particularly efficient since it would have required two or three men to lift the completed motorcycle.**

ABOVE: **By 1924, there were 500,000 motorcycles registered in Britain and although it was hardly typical of what was available during the Depression, the British manufacturer BSA had started to produce the 770cc V-twin Model G14 in 1921. Available in solo and sidecar combination form, it was popular with ex-servicemen.** RIGHT: **In Germany during the 1930s, light motorcycles, with engines under 350cc, were typically produced by BMW, DKW, NSU and TWN (Triumph).**

of comparative trials. At the end of the trials, the Matchless T/4, AJS M6 and Douglas L29 were considered to be suitable for further testing but eventually it was concluded that no civilian machine would be suitable and that MWEE should design a purpose-made military motorcycle. The only useful outcome of the trials was probably the standardization of the layout of motorcycle controls.

There never was a purpose-designed British military motorcycle but BSA's 500cc, so-called WD Twin, was procured in large numbers from around 1934.

Elsewhere, the closing of the 1920s and the early years of the new decade were a period of expansion, with new manufacturers springing up across the world. In the Soviet Union, the Izhevsk Steel Plant launched five new motorcycles in 1928, with lighter Soviet machines beginning to appear in 1930. With restricted domestic potential, the machines found a ready use with the Red Army.

The Polish CWS state workshops started manufacturing motorcycles in 1930, the M-III of 1933 being particularly suited to military use. In the newly created Czechoslovakia, there were eventually something like 120 motorcycle manufacturers, and companies such as CZ, Jawa, Ogar, Praga, and Itar & Walter supplied both military and civilian machines. Japan copied the big Harley-Davidson V-twin to produce the Sankyo *Shinagawa* Rikuo 97 in 1937. The Italian Moto-Guzzi, Gilera and Benelli companies were all established during the mid-1930s and their products were widely used by the Italian Army. In France, Peugeot, Gnome & Rhône, René Gillet, Mercier, and Terrot supplied heavy motorcycles to the French Army, while the Belgian FN, and Gillet-Herstal companies pioneered the driven-wheel sidecar outfits which were later to be used so successfully by the *Wehrmacht*. The Swedish company Husqvarna had started supplying the Swedish Army from the early 1920s.

In Germany, the motorcycle industry had been well established by 1920. Victoria had started motorcycle

production in 1899, and NSU in 1901; Zündapp, Ardie and DKW had been building motorcycles since 1919. Newcomer, BMW produced the first motorcycle under its own name in 1923. As the Third Reich increased the production of consumer goods as a way of improving the average German's standard of living, motorcycle production increased year on year. More than 200,000 motorcycles were produced between 1934 and 1939, and many of these civilian machines eventually found their way into military service.

The USA was keen to never again become involved in a European conflict, and had imposed its isolationist strategy. Although, for a period, there was a plan to issue every newly graduated GI with a motorcycle, the Great Depression brought such notions to an abrupt end. Civilian motorcycle sales declined sharply during the inter-war years – in 1929 for example just 96,400 motorcycles were sold in the USA – and although both Indian and Harley-Davidson machines were purchased by the US Army, it was in small numbers, and export orders to both sides in the Spanish Civil War and to China made little difference. However, everything changed in 1939.

ABOVE: **After 1931, Harley-Davidson and Indian became the only surviving volume motorcycle manufacturers in the USA, with Harley being the larger. These lads are mounted on a Harley-Davidson Model JD.**

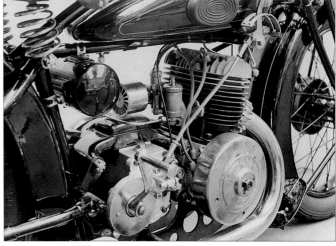

Increasing sophistication and reliability

During the inter-war period, motorcycle development progressed in leaps and bounds, and the 1920s and 1930s might be considered by many as the golden age of motorcycling as the machines became faster and more reliable. Although rear suspension did not become a standard feature until the post-war period, engines became more powerful and side valves began to be replaced by overhead valves. Lubrication was hugely improved as engine-driven pumps, in combination with a proper sump, ousted the early hand pumps and total-loss systems that had been common in the early days. Belt drive disappeared completely and the old two- and three-speed gearboxes with clumsy hand change levers started to be replaced by four-speed units, often with a slick foot-pedal operation. Brakes were universally fitted to both front and rear wheels and had been improved beyond measure.

ABOVE LEFT AND ABOVE: **During the late 1920s, J.S. Ramussen's DKW Zschopauer Motorenwerke had become the largest motorcycle manufacturer in the world. In 1927, the company exhibited this DKW motorcycle at London's Motorcycle Show at Olympia.**

New manufacturers continued to emerge, some of them offering ever-more sophisticated machinery, and the mid-to-late 1930s saw some of the most innovative designs in motorcycling, albeit many of these were more expensive. At the same time, in Britain and Europe, the motorcycle continued to be seen as an inexpensive alternative to public transport or a step up from the pedal cycle and many manufacturers also exploited this utilitarian trend.

DKW was established in Germany in 1919, specializing in two-strokes, Horex produced its first motorcycle in 1923, and

LEFT: **As this photograph shows, Adolf Hitler very much believed that both military and sporting success might help the German nation to regain its pride. The motorcycle is a racing BMW.**

LEFT AND BELOW:
A factory to assemble Triumph motorcycles in Germany was established in 1903. During the inter-war years the machines were badged as TWN (Triumph Werke Nürnberg). Shown is a 350cc model of 1935.

Maico was established in 1935. Two names which were later to be associated with powerful and sophisticated military motorcycles – Zündapp and BMW – were established in 1921 and 1923, respectively. In Italy, Benelli started production in 1917 and soon made a name for itself with fast road-going and racing machines, notably incorporating water cooling. Moto-Guzzi was created in 1921 and, within two years, was producing racing machines using overhead camshafts. Jawa started production of a sophisticated shaft-driven 500cc machine in Czechoslovakia in 1929; CZ following in 1932 with a range of lightweight machines with tiny engines and pressed-steel frames. The French Motobécane company started producing motorcycles in 1923, producing a high-quality in-line four-cylinder machine with a unit gearbox and shaft drive, later becoming France's largest manufacturer.

In Britain, well-established marques such as BSA, Matchless, Ariel and Triumph dominated the market, but it seemed that there was always room for a newcomer. For example the advanced JAP-engined HRDs first appearing in 1924, and the high-quality Vincent, with its unique rear suspension, was first marketed in 1928.

While the civilian motorcycle became increasingly powerful and sophisticated during these inter-war years, there remained a steady market for more utilitarian military machines. It may be true that the military were never afraid to try something new – witness the curious three-wheeled and tracked machines that the War Office in Britain thoroughly tested in the late 1920s – but the machines that were purchased in quantity tended to be very conventional. One exception to this rule was the concept of the driven sidecar wheel, which was developed in Belgium as a means of providing a heavy military motorcycle which could travel literally anywhere. The Belgian FN, Gillet and Sarolea companies all produced such machines during 1937/38 and, of course, the concept was subsequently adopted enthusiastically by the *Wehrmacht* during World War II.

Although steady from the mid-1920s, European military procurement of motorcycles started to gather pace as many nations embarked on rearmament programmes.

In the USA, the combination of the low-priced utilitarian Ford Model T followed by the Great Depression had a serious impact on motorcycle sales. Excelsior and Henderson both closed in 1931, leaving just Harley-Davidson and Indian. Both companies continued to produce high-quality well-built machines but they did not sell in large numbers on the domestic market and high tariffs prevented them reaching the European markets. Only the US police services remained loyal to the big US machines during this period – as even the military reduced expenditure on motorcycles. It was probably sport which helped to save the US motorcycle industry as the machines became a favourite of enthusiasts and amateur racers during the 1930s.

Tracked motorcycles

During World War I, four-wheel drive vehicles were something of a rarity, and motorcycles were employed for their ability to make headway on unmade roads and across ground that was pockmarked with craters from the incessant shelling. Nevertheless, the damage to the ground was often so severe that even a motorcycle was unable to make progress and, in the same way that automotive engineers began to experiment with four- and six-wheel drive and with the use of half-track systems in the years following World War I, so motorcycles also came under the spotlight.

One of the first attempts at improving the traction of the motorcycle came in 1923, when the US Army tested an Indian Chief, which had been fitted with a Chase track system. The rear wheel was pushed further back by the use of a sub-frame and a chain was used to drive a cleated canvas track wrapped around the rear wheel, with an idler wheel to control tension and to extend the length of the track in contact with the ground. The system had been used on Dodge and Ford vehicles the year before, but had proved unsuitable for military use.

During the 1920s, the British Army believed that the 6x4 drive-line layout offered almost as good a performance as the 4x4 (or 6x6) without the mechanical complexity. Mechanics of the Royal Army Service Corps (RASC) attempted to produce what might be described as a 3x2 motorcycle by adapting a Triumph Model P to mount a bogie at the rear which carried a pair of in-line wheels. The first wheel was chain-driven by a sprocket; on the other side of this wheel,

TOP, ABOVE AND BELOW: **Following the modification of a Triumph Model P by RASC mechanics, the British company OEC produced three versions of this unlikely three-wheeled motorcycle which was described as a "tractor". A flexible track could be wrapped around the rear wheels, both of which were driven, to improve traction.**

a pulley was fitted which drove the second wheel by means of a substantial V belt. If extra traction was required, a track could be fitted around these wheels. The prototype was submitted for trials during 1926 and apparently performed well across soft ground, and reasonably well on tarmac. There was a tendency for the rearmost wheel to lift as the bogie responded to power, and cornering on tarmac must have been interesting, but the machine was considered to have sufficient potential for further development and the project was passed to OEC in 1928.

OEC was selected to continue the development work since it had a reputation as a manufacturer of "custom" motorcycles and during 1927/28 three further prototypes were produced which OEC confusingly described as a "caterpillar tractor". Two of the machines were powered by a 350cc Blackburne engine, the third used a 490cc JAP; all three employed a variation of the in-line bogie at the rear which had been devised by the RASC. The trials were eventually abandoned with the War Office concluding that the added complexity did not outweigh the increase in off-road performance.

In 1936, the Swiss (or French) Mercier company built a prototype of a JAP-engined half-tracked motorcycle – or *moto-chenille* – in which the track was fitted at the front. The engine was mounted ahead over the handlebars and the four-wheel bogie was driven via an exposed chain. It was tested by the French Army and then by the British War Office in 1939 but was considered to be slow, unwieldy, uncomfortable and unsafe. Surprisingly, the machine still exists.

The only successful tracked motorcycle design was the German *Kettenkrad* but so little of the machine was derived from the motorcycle that it probably does not really count.

Finally, although not tracked, it is worth mentioning the Rokon motorcycle developed by Californian inventor Charles Fehn. Fehn set out to build the ultimate off-road lightweight motorcycle and, by combining full-time two-wheel drive, with an automatic transmission and high-flotation hollow wheels, the Rokon delivers unrivalled performance across virtually every type of terrain.

ABOVE: **Built by NSU, the German *Kettenkrad* is probably the world's only successful tracked motorcycle, albeit much of the technology is derived from the *Wehrmacht*'s conventional half-tracked vehicles.**
LEFT: **The Rokon motorcycle, developed by Charles Fehn, includes two-wheel drive and automatic transmission.**

Military Motorcycles from World War II to the Present Day

After the end of World War I, military motorcycles continued to play an important role in strategic thinking, with the motorcycle-mounted *Kradschützen* troops forming a significant element of the German Blitzkrieg lightning assault tactic in World War II. However, the introduction of the Jeep in 1941 highlighted the motorcycle's limitations and, by the end of the war, motorcycles were being used mainly in Military Police and convoy escort duties.

There was some resurgence of motorcycle use towards the end of the 20th century, as desert warfare demanded off-road machines and ATVs. Indeed, by the end of the 1950s, all of the elements of the modern motorcycle were in place. Developments since then have seen incredible increases in engine power and machine performance and reliability. The first diesel-powered motorcycles appeared in 2001.

This chapter examines the history of the military motorcycle from World War II to the present day. Special topics include motorcycles in combat, the heavy and lightweight motorcycles of World War II, folding and airborne motorcycles, motor tricycles, ATVs and quad bikes. There is also a country-by-country overview of military motorcycles in France, Belgium, Germany, Italy, Great Britain, the USA, the USSR and Japan.

LEFT: **With a powerful engine, selectable sidecar-wheel drive and often low-ratio cross-country gears, the big German combination outfits of World War II probably represent the pinnacle of heavy military motorcycle design. Shown is the BMW R-12, a militarized civilian model.**

ABOVE: **Although this photograph of massed infantry motorcyclists might suggest otherwise, the British tended to confine the motorcycle to the messenger role during World War II.**

ABOVE AND BELOW: **Nazi Germany saw the motorcycle, particularly when combined with a military sidecar, as a legitimate tool of the Blitzkrieg tactic and even mounted machine-guns on sidecars, a carry over from World War I.**

Deployment of the motorcycle in World War II

Huge numbers of motorcycles were constructed and deployed by the opposing nations during World War II (1939–45). Total Allied production amounted to something like 530,000 machines during this period; of these, 425,000 were built in the UK, with the majority of the remainder coming from Indian and Harley-Davidson in the USA. During those same years Germany – including Austria – produced 305,640 machines, of which some 80,000 were supplied to civilians, although many were subsequently requisitioned by the military. The Germans also used captured and requisitioned machines produced in France and Belgium. Thousands more motorcycles were produced in Italy and Japan.

Clearly, for all sides of what was the first fully mechanized conflict, motorcycles were an important element and the machines were deployed across all the combat theatres as well as being widely used for domestic duties. Typical roles for the motorcycle included despatch riding, personnel transport, and reconnaissance; motorcycles were also used by military police units, and in traffic control and convoy escort duties.

Despatch riding had been the first significant military use for the motorcycle during World War I, and motorcycles had been used to carry vital messages, orders, maps and documents between often geographically separated locations. Despite the widespread growth in radio and electronic signals traffic, despatch riding remained a vital role during World War II and still remains the most important role for the military motorcycle.

The relative mobility of the motorcycle compared to the primitive motor trucks of the period had ensured that the transportation of personnel in the field was also a significant role during World War I. Two decades later, Allied officers were more likely to be found riding in a staff car behind the lines and, if the going got rough, the vehicle of choice was almost certainly going to be a Jeep. Nevertheless, the Germans often favoured the motorcycle combination as a form of personnel carrier, and even among the Allies the sidecar still had its uses both for transporting personnel and moving vital cargo where other transport might, perhaps, be unable to proceed.

ABOVE: **Although the riders are in typical British tropical uniform, the motorcycles are strictly civilian overhead valve Triumphs, probably the T80 Tigers which remained in production until 1939.**
LEFT: **A British despatch rider posing in front of a Vickers medium tank.**

The motorcycle was also the ideal mount for reconnaissance forces. The small size and relative unobtrusiveness of a solo motorcycle will often allow it to approach closer to enemy positions than a larger armoured vehicle, while the speed and manoeuvrability of the machine also allows a quick retreat should this be necessary. Motorcycle reconnaissance units were typically used to report on the condition of roads, to locate and report on the strength of enemy units, and to call in the accuracy of artillery fire.

Behind the lines, motorcycles were widely deployed for traffic control and convoy escort duties. A number of motorcycles accompanying a typical convoy were able to

ABOVE: **Mounted on Victoria KR6 heavy sidecar combinations, these German motorcycle troops – *Kradschüdtzen* – are masked against the dust.**
RIGHT: **The Norton Big Four, complete with a driven sidecar wheel, was a British Army experiment with a heavy motorcycle in the German style. It was not a success and was replaced by the American Jeep.**

weave around and move ahead of a column of vehicles, keeping the road clear and ensuring that stragglers did not become separated from the main body of the convoy. And by riding ahead of the convoy, opposing or cross traffic could be held up as necessary to allow a convoy to pass through a major intersection as a unit.

Military police and border guards were frequently motorcycle mounted, patrolling bases and off-limits areas to ensure that night-time and security restrictions were observed. The US Navy used motorcycles for shore patrols in the same way.

The German and Soviet armies were alone in making widespread use of motorcycles as a fighting part of a combat unit; these roles are dealt with separately. The Allies also assigned motorcycles to both infantry and armour divisions – a US division during World War II, for example, might have had 200 motorcycles available, but they were used exclusively in an administrative or reconnaissance role.

Unlike the previous conflict, motorcycles were no longer used as stretcher carriers, although the *Wehrmacht* certainly mounted medical staff on motorcycle combinations, nor were they used to mount radios or carry pigeons.

Motorcycles in combat

The Germans employed their elite motorcycle troops – the so-called *Kradschützen* – with great effect during the Blitzkrieg campaigns of the early years of World War II, where they could be considered as mechanized cavalry, forming part of the highly mobile and hard-hitting spearhead units. Even the reconnaissance *Abteilung* (battalion) included motorcycle-mounted combat troops who were willing and able to fight should the opportunity or need arise.

The Germans were almost alone in their widespread use of motorcycle combat troops. The Red Army used small numbers of motorcycles as part of their hybrid cavalry-mechanized groups, neither the British nor the US armies chose to copy this tactic, preferring instead to restrict motorcycles to the reconnaissance, despatch rider and administrative roles – although it must be pointed out that motorcycles did feature in a number of airborne operations. It was not always thus.

In the inter-war years, the strategic planners of the US Marine Corps saw little future for the military motorcycle, preferring to concentrate on the use of "cross-country cars" for reconnaissance duties and arguing that the motorcycle had a limited range and was restricted to "fairly good roads".

On the other hand, the US Army envisaged motorcycle-mounted troops speeding out in front of advancing columns of armour and reporting on the enemy's strengths and positions. As late as 1941, for example, the US 2nd Cavalry Division was equipped with horses, scout cars, Jeeps and motorcycles. Sadly, a man mounted on a solo motorcycle can do little to defend himself – he generally needs both hands to control the machine and has little opportunity to fire at a pursuer or at enemy units upon which he may have stumbled. Nevertheless, US Signal Corps photographs from the late 1930s show US infantrymen

ABOVE: **Clearly, a motorcycle, in this case a BSA M20, can provide a useful vantage point even if this is not quite what was meant by motorcycle reconnaissance.**

in training, wearing full-face masks against the clouds of dust thrown up by their own machines, they can be seen hurling their big Harley-Davidson or Indian motorcycles on to the ground and crouching behind them with carbines raised. Other training shots show columns of motorcycles operating alongside Jeeps and armoured scout cars but, in practice, the US Army motorcyclist was rarely part of a front-line combat unit.

In Britain, too, the years before the widespread appearance of the Jeep saw the War Office continuing to develop the combat role of the motorcycle combination by mounting a

LEFT: **The Germans were almost alone in their widespread use of motorcycles for combat troops – these *Kradschützen* head-up a convoy of military vehicles in what is almost certainly an exhibition of power and authority.**

machine-gun on a special sidecar. More than 4,700 Norton
Big Four sidecar outfits were procured between 1938 and 1942
and one of its envisaged roles was to provide an all-terrain
mount for both reconnaissance and combat units. The sidecar
body could also be removed and replaced by a tripod-mounted
mortar. The Jeep put an end to these ideas and the motorcycle
was generally relegated to behind-the-lines roles.

The French and Belgian armies had also come round to the
idea that motorcycle troops could replace cavalry units during
the inter-war years but neither nation had any opportunity to
put these ideas into practice.

The Italian Army toyed with mounting machine-guns on
the distinctive motor tricycles produced by Gilera, Moto-
Guzzi and Benelli but they were almost certainly never in
widespread use with combat troops. It was a similar story
in Japan where machine-guns were frequently mounted on
motorcycles but rarely used as a combat tactic.

In common with the Germans, although on a much smaller
scale, the Soviets considered motorcycle troops to be a vital
component of combat units and included motorcycle battalions
in the Red Army Order of Battle even as late as mid-1944. For
example, during the latter stages of the fighting on the Eastern
Front, the 30th Motorcycle Regiment had been used as part of

ABOVE LEFT: **The Germans also used motorcycle combinations to provide transport for the lower ranks of officers.**
ABOVE: **British motorcycle outriders accompanying a mixed convoy of vehicles. Note the Jeep behind the Bren carrier.** RIGHT: **Motorcycle riders were easily thrown from their mounts or even decapitated by a wire stretched across the road at a strategic height. Like Jeeps, motorcycles were frequently fitted with some means of deflecting and breaking the wire.**

the Soviet mixed cavalry-mechanized group. The tactic
involved using the armoured and motorized formations of the
mechanized corps to provide the main combat power, while
the horse-mounted elements provided flexibility for fighting in
difficult terrain such as large forests, or waterlogged ground.

LEFT: **The US Army developed this technique for using motorcycles as cover for infantrymen but it is doubtful that the tactic was ever used in anger. If nothing else, a motorcycle would have been very vulnerable to enemy fire, leaving the rider stranded.**

47

Kradschützen – elite motorcycle troops

In mechanizing their army, the German High Command placed considerable importance on the rapid mobility of the motorcycle. The so-called *Kradschützen*, or motorcycle infantrymen – often called *Kradmelder* (despatch riders) – were a vital part of the German Blitzkrieg tactic and were considered to be elite troops. Using the principle of "fire and movement", and exploiting the superiority in speed and movement available from the motorcycle, their role was to surprise and outflank the enemy far ahead of own armoured forces.

The German *Reichswehr* had formed its first motorcycle infantry company in 1929, and further motorcycle infantry units were formed during 1934/35, mainly by restructuring former cavalry regiments. Although their equipment and weapons were light, and the lightly modified and requisitioned civilian motorcycles of the period were often lacking in reliability, these units were very effective in combat, proving their worth during the campaigns in France and Poland.

However, the shortcomings of these essentially civilian machines became all too obvious, and it was clear that a

ABOVE: **Heavy motorcycle combinations were produced for the** *Wehrmacht* **by Zündapp and BMW, both companies also producing a version with a driven wheel to the sidecar.** ABOVE RIGHT: **Dating from 1937, the single-cylinder BMW R-35 was widely used for training, despatch and liaison duties.** RIGHT: **The horizontally opposed engine has become something of a BMW trademark and, although lacking sidecar drive, the 750cc R-12 was typical of the German heavy motorcycle of World War II.**

purpose-designed military motorcycle was the only way forward. The *Wehrmacht* had already been purchasing the Zündapp KS600-W heavy combination outfit since 1938, eventually acquiring some 18,000 of these machines, but the big Zündapp was also to provide the basis for a new, powerful and specialized military machine with all-wheel drive.

Development work on the Zündapp KS750, and the similar BMW R-75, started in April 1940, with the first machines introduced in the autumn of 1940 during the North African campaign. Both machines were designed to be able to transport three men together with their equipment, and could also double as a prime mover for airborne light artillery or tow a light trailer. The notion of driving the sidecar wheel had been developed in France and Belgium where various manufacturers had been producing such machines since the mid-1930s – but by combining this with other features, Zündapp and BMW produced a state-of-the-art heavy military motorcycle, albeit at a cost which exceeded that of the *Kübelwagen*.

With their sidecar-wheel drive, low-ratio cross-country gears, and reverse – the BMW even featured a lockable differential – these machines provided a cross-country performance that often exceeded that of the US-built Jeep.

An *Einheits* (standard) design of single-seat sidecar was used, with stowage for a spare wheel, ammunition and fuel, and with provision for a radio; a light mortar was also occasionally carried. A pintle mount was often fitted on the nose of the sidecar, allowing an MG-34 or MG-42 machine-gun to be fired on the move.

More than 35,000 of these heavy motorcycles were constructed by the two companies between 1940 and 1944 but, for the motorcycles which had performed so well in Africa and on the Western Front, it was a very different story when Germany turned to the East.

On June 22, 1941, Germany launched "Operation Barbarossa", the invasion of the Soviet Union where they faced, not only the might of the Red Army but the appalling conditions of the Russian winter. With the autumn rains, the roads turned into impassable bogs and the land became a sea of apparently bottomless oozing mud. When a motorcycle could be persuaded to move, more often than not it was defeated by the liquid mud which was ingested by the intake system. Motorized forces were reduced to travelling less than 16km/10 miles a day. The arrival of winter heralded plumetting temperatures – at minus 40°C (-40°F), the engine and transmission oil virtually froze solid. Some lucky soldiers benefited from the special foot and hand warming systems that were fitted to their motorcycles, others simply froze to death.

BMW sent engineers to the Front to see, first hand, how the motorcycles fared but, there was little that could be done. The German war machine ground to a halt at Stalingrad and never recovered – even the elite *Kradschützen* were simply overwhelmed by the Russian winter.

ABOVE: **Both BMW and Zündapp adopted the pressed-steel external frame. Wearing the *Kradmantel*, this German soldier seems to have attracted something of a crowd of onlookers around his mud-encrusted machine.** BELOW: **German *Kradschützen* at rest: the motorcycles that can be identified appear to be BMW R-12s. The helmets and rifles suggest that the troops are waiting for orders to deploy.**

Motorcycle design during World War II

By 1939, motorcycle design was well into what might be termed its second phase. A specific design language had started to emerge and, although the machines no longer resembled pedal cycles, the high-tech revolution started by the Japanese was still some years into the future. Where the 1930s had been a time of innovation, the war brought this to an end, and the emphasis was placed firmly on volume production. In Britain and the USA particularly, the manufacturers produced what were essentially militarized pre-war civilian machines throughout the long years of the conflict and, despite some British and US experiments in this direction, only in Germany was there any serious attempt made to produce a purpose-designed military motorcycle.

Regardless of origin, military motorcycles can be considered to fall broadly into three categories – nicely summed up by the always-orderly Germans, following one of the Schell rationalization programmes, as "lightweight", "medium weight" and "heavy weight". Machines in the upper end of the medium-weight category and heavy-weight machines were equally suitable for solo or sidecar use although, with the notable exception of Germany, sidecars were generally less favoured than had been the case during World War I.

Lightweight machines, some of which were specifically designed for use by airborne troops, were powered by a single-cylinder engine of less than 250cc, either of the two-stroke or four-stroke type. Most British motorcycles, and the more numerous of the German models, fell into the medium-weight category, these employing an engine of between 250cc and 500cc, and again generally of single-cylinder design. Motorcycles in the third category, typically produced by Germany and the USA, were powered by an engine of more than 500cc, often of twin-cylinder design. The Germans invariably used the horizontally opposed "boxer" layout, while the US-built Indian and Harley-Davidson companies favoured the V-twin.

ABOVE: **Germany annexed Austria in 1938 and used large numbers of Puch motorcycles throughout World War II, as well as Austrian-built trucks.**
BELOW: **It was not only the rigours of combat that shortened the life of the motorcycle – competitive use away from the front line also caused damage.**

Side-valve engines still tended to predominate, although most manufacturers were well aware of the performance advantages of overhead valves, and even overhead camshafts. Most machines continued to use magneto ignition although there were advantages to the use of the battery-and-coil system. Notwithstanding Indian's early experiments with electric starting, which had almost bankrupted the company, inertia kick starting remained the norm.

Japanese and Soviet designers tended to follow US practice but Italy produced the most exotic designs of the conflict. For example, Moto-Guzzi, uniquely, stuck with their pre-war exposed

ABOVE: **Although the weight and unfamiliar controls counted against it, RAF motorcyclists found the Indian 741B motorcycle to be reliable and comfortable.**

flywheel and single horizontal cylinder engine, and Benelli used overhead camshafts. Alone among the European armies, Italy also favoured a widespread use of three-wheeled motor tricycles, as did the Japanese in the Far East.

Except for the very smallest airborne lightweight motorcycles, a multi-speed transmission was the norm. A handful of ultra-lightweights might have used a two-speed transmission, but for most there was a proper three or four-speed gearbox. British motorcycles tended to favour a foot change for the gearbox but the Germans and the Americans were just as likely to employ a tank-mounted hand-change lever. Belt drive had been discontinued back in World War I and final drive was normally by means of a roller chain, although BMW and Zündapp, particularly, tended to favour shaft drive for their purpose-designed military machines.

Sidecar wheel drive had been pioneered in the UK for trials racing in the 1930s, and the concept was subsequently adopted for specialized military machines produced by Belgian motorcycle manufacturers FN, Sarolea and Gillet-Herstal at the end of the 1930s. In Germany, Zündapp, and then BMW,

produced heavy military motorcycles from 1940 that incorporated drive to the sidecar wheel as well as having low-ratio gears to aid cross-country work.

There was little innovation in suspension design. From the earliest days of motorcycle design, front suspension had quickly become a standard feature, almost invariably by means of friction-damped coil springs and girder parallelogram forks and this remained the norm. There were a few exceptions to this, with some BMWs and Zündapps and Britain's Matchless G3L notably using telescopic forks. It was still unusual for the rear forks to be sprung.

As shortages of materials, notably rubber and aluminium, became apparent, manufacturers were forced to adopt substitutes. In Britain and the USA, for example, rubber was in short supply due to Japanese action in the Far East, and this led to the adoption of canvas handlebar grips and cast-steel footrests rather than the previous rubber-cushioned type; unnecessary rubber items such as knee pads were eliminated. Aluminium was essential for aircraft production and items such as primary chain cases, and even crankcases, which had previously been cast in aluminium, were often remanufactured in steel or cast iron.

Motorcycles remained in production by all of the major combatants throughout the conflict but there is no doubt that their role became less significant, and certainly more mundane, after the appearance of lightweight all-terrain vehicles such as the US-built Jeep and the German *Kübelwagen*.

BELOW: **During World War II, advances in technology took second place to reliability but even so, the life of a motorcycle on the front line was often very short. These Italian outriders are mounted on typical lightweight machines of the period.**

Heavy motorcycles of World War II

During World War II, the heaviest military motorcycles were those fitted with an engine larger than 500cc, together with drive to the sidecar wheel. This excludes virtually all of the British motorcycles of the period since most were fitted with engines of 350cc or just under 500cc and few were used with sidecars at all. It also eliminates all of the US-built Harley-Davidsons and Indians which, although they were almost universally powered by large engines, were never provided with sidecar wheel drive. So, the category really only includes the British Norton 633cc Big Four and the big Zündapp and BMW sidecar outfits favoured by combat units of the *Wehrmacht*.

It is probably no coincidence that the Norton Big Four falls into the same category as the Zündapps and BMWs since it was almost certainly inspired by the same big Belgian outfits as the German machines.

ABOVE: **The side-valve BMW R-12 was typical of German heavy motorcycles until the production of more capable machines with sidecar drive in 1940.**

ABOVE: **The use of selectable sidecar wheel drive, and even limited-slip differentials, gave the later German outfits a formidable off-road performance.** LEFT: **While the heavy German motorcycles were frequently used in combat, lighter machines, like this 200cc pressed-frame DKW, were used in their thousands behind the lines.**

LEFT: **With its horizontally opposed engine, front suspension and shaft drive, the Harley-Davidson XA was an American attempt at producing a heavy motorcycle in the German style. It was originally intended for deployment in the Western Desert but came too late and it is doubtful that any saw overseas' service.**

The Belgian FN company had produced its first 3x2 sidecar outfit, the M12-SM, in 1937, and the British War Department would certainly have known of its existence. In 1938, a second Belgian company, Gillet-Herstal, also produced a similar heavy motorcycle with selectable drive to the sidecar wheel and in 1939, at the request of the Belgian company, one of these outfits was pitched head-to-head with the then-new Norton Big Four at the British Mechanical Warfare Engineering Establishment (MWEE).

The Norton Big Four was a development of the company's 16H which had first been trialled with sidecar wheel drive in 1938. Although it is said to have been inspired partly by a competition trials outfit, it is inconceivable that the design was not also influenced by the developments in Belgium. The engine was a huge 633cc single-cylinder unit in combination with a four-speed forward and reverse gearbox, and drive to the sidecar wheel was via a dog clutch. Performance was said to be excellent across country and the machine was intended to be used by combat troops, with a machine-gun mounted on the sidecar in the style of the German Blitzkrieg units. Following the trials, the Gillet-Herstal machine was not felt to offer any particular advantages and the Norton Big Four was approved for production, with some 4,737 examples produced during the period 1938 to 1942. It was never really used as intended and many examples were disposed of on the civilian market after the appearance of the Jeep in 1941, albeit with the sidecar drive disconnected.

Meanwhile, the *Wehrmacht* had almost certainly appropriated FN, Sarolea and Gillet-Herstal 3x2 motorcycles from the Belgian Army after 1940 and would have been well aware of the advantages of such a system. When the rigours of service in the Western Desert exposed the weaknesses of existing German motorcycle outfits, Zündapp was asked to design a powerful military motorcycle which could withstand the desert conditions. The result was the Zündapp KS750 combination outfit. Design features included the elimination of the troublesome roller chain in favour of shaft drive, a forward and reverse gearbox with a low-

ABOVE: **Although it lacked rear suspension, the Zündapp KS750 was possibly the most advanced motorcycle used by any of the combatants during World War II. Features included telescopic front suspension, overhead-valve engine, shaft drive, forward/reverse gearbox and sidecar drive.**

ratio crawler gear for off-road use, selectable sidecar wheel drive, hydraulic brakes on the sidecar and rear wheel, high-level exhaust, and high-efficiency air filters. Production started in 1940.

BMW's R-75, also first produced in 1940, shared many of these features and, with its three-speed plus overdrive main gearbox and two-speed auxiliary gearbox, also offered almost a full set of low-ratio gears. Curiously, neither machine featured rear suspension although both had telescopic front forks.

These were not cheap machines, with the price said to be higher than that of the VW *Kübelwagen*, and production of both was eventually cancelled in 1944 after 18,635 KS750s and 16,510 R-75s had been manufactured.

As for the US "heavies", it is not quite fair to eliminate them entirely since there were trials of the Harley-Davidson XA with a driven sidecar, as well as possibly a prototype WLA with a driven sidecar wheel intended for the Soviet Army but there was no production of either.

Lightweight motorcycles of World War II

With the amount of attention that is directed at the US-built Harley-Davidsons and Indians, and the big German motorcycles of World War II, there is an understandable tendency to believe that these heavy machines were typical of motorcycles in military use. In fact, both sides used large numbers of relatively lightweight machines, typically for liaison duties and in the airborne role.

The big Zündapp and BMW sidecar machines were not produced in massive numbers and there were many, many more lightweight machines in *Wehrmacht* service. In fact, the only German motorcycle to remain in production for the entire duration of the war was the small DKW RT-125, essentially a pre-war civilian machine powered by a single-cylinder two-stroke engine and fit only for light duties; unladen weight was 91kg/200lb. DKW also produced an even smaller machine, the 98cc RT-3 that was widely used by *Wehrmacht*.

Similar lightweight machines were produced by Ardie, in the form of the RBZ200 and the VF125, at 197cc and 125cc, respectively, and by Phänomen whose 124cc AHOI entered service in 1938. Even Zündapp produced a lightweight 125cc machine, the DBK-200 Derby of 1935, which was used by the *Wehrmacht*. Other lightweight commercial machines came from the Czech Ogar, Jawa and CZ factories, none of them with engines larger than 350cc.

British motorcycles of World War II tended to be 250cc or 350cc side-valve machines, but these were certainly not the whole story. Even if you disregard the specialist lightweight airborne machines, which are dealt with separately, the British Army employed a total of more than 14,500 lightweights produced by James and Royal Enfield.

Nicknamed the "Clockwork Mouse", the 125cc James ML was first manufactured in 1943 and, with folding handlebars and footrests, it was originally intended for use by airborne and assault units, although it was subsequently widely used by

ABOVE: **Lightweight motorcycles were popular in Germany and were produced by Ardie, DKW, Phänomen, and NSU.** BELOW: **Lightweight civilian machines, often unmodified, were frequently used for training purposes.**

ABOVE AND BELOW: **The James ML "Clockwork Mouse" was intended for use by airborne and assault units and featured folding handlebars and footrests.**

to European eyes, it was an almost conventional lightweight motorcycle. Procured in limited numbers for use by airborne troops during 1943, it was a militarized version of the company's Powercycle and was powered by a 194cc two-stroke engine with belt drive to the rear wheel via a twin pulley arrangement that gave the rider a choice of two gears; top speed was 50kph/30mph. The weight was quoted at 75kg/165lb.

The US Army also procured examples of the Indian Aerocycle, which was designated "extra light solo motorcycle M1 – standard". It was standardized in December 1944 and, again, was intended largely for use by airborne troops. The engine was a single-cylinder 221cc unit that gave a top speed of 73kph/45mph, and the machine was also said to be suitable for off-road use. With a total unladen weight of 114kg/250lb it was around half the weight of a standard US Army Harley-Davidson or Indian machine and could be lightened further by removing the battery – the ignition was a magneto design – lights and generator. This brought the weight down 114kg/250lb but nevertheless it did not compare well to, for example, the British James ML or Royal Enfield WD/RE.

Lightweight motorcycles, including mopeds and scooters, were also widely used by all nations in the post-war years.

Commandos and ground forces. Powered by a small single-cylinder Villiers engine installed in a lightweight tubular frame, it was not dissimilar to the lightweight DKWs, and weighed in at just 72kg/157lb. The Royal Enfield WD/RE of 1942 – better known as the "Flying Flea" – was based on a lightweight pre-war civilian motorcycle, which, in turn, is said to have been derived from the German-built DKW RT-98. With a 125cc single-cylinder engine, it was similar to the James ML but at 62kg/137lb it had a 9kg/20lb weight advantage, and tended to be favoured for use by airborne assault troops where it was air-dropped in a special protective cradle.

Even the USA had a choice of lightweight machines at their disposal. The Simplex Servi-Cycle was described by the Ordnance Corps as a "motor-driven bicycle" although,

ABOVE: **Indian produced this "extra light" solo machine, described as the Aerocycle Model 144, or 148, according to the date of manufacture. It was also intended for airborne use.**
RIGHT: **German *Hitler-Jugend* demonstrate some unusual uses for a lightweight motorcycle at a training camp in the late 1930s.**

Folding and airborne motorcycles

The emergence of airborne troops that could be inserted behind enemy lines by either parachute or glider also demanded a new approach to the design of equipment. The troops could not be heavily equipped, but needed sufficient in terms of firepower and mobility to complete their allotted tasks. Foot power was all very well, but there were limits to how far troops could travel under their own power. In Britain, Jeeps were adapted for airborne use but were restricted to glider delivery while, at the other end of the scale, folding airborne bicycles were produced both in Britain and the USA.

However, motorcycles seemed to offer a good compromise. Providing it was protected by a suitable enclosure or container,

ABOVE: **British paratroopers loading a Jeep and motorcycles into an early type Airspeed Horsa assault glider.** ABOVE LEFT: **The US Cushman Autoglide 53 was designed for air-dropping.**

even a standard lightweight civilian motorcycle could be air-dropped alongside paratroops, and could provide some mobility in the early hours or days of an airborne assault. British airborne doctrine held that if key individuals in an operation were mobilized it would speed the movement of messages between elements of, what could often be a widely dispersed, airborne operation.

Produced from 1942, the British Royal Enfield WD/RE "Flying Flea" and the James ML were both lightweight, expendable – for

ABOVE: **The British James ML was sufficiently lightweight to permit easy manhandling.** RIGHT: **The Excelsior Welbike was also light enough to be easily lifted into an aircraft.**

which read "low-cost" – machines considered to be suitable for air-dropping in a specially designed cradle, or for being carried in a glider. Both of these were lightweight civilian machines that had been adapted for a military role, but the Excelsior Welbike was designed from the start as a lightweight airborne machine.

The Welbike was designed to provide a simple, lightweight expendable motorcycle that could be reduced in size to fit into a standard air-drop container. Powered by a 98cc two-stroke Villiers engine, the prototype was produced by J. R. V. Dolphin at Welwyn – hence the name – with development work taking place at the Airborne Forces Experimental Establishment (AFEE). It was designed around a tubular space frame that allowed the handlebars and saddle to be folded or collapsed to reduce the overall height and, with small wheels and compact automotive layout, could be stowed inside a cylindrical container. The container, incidentally could also be fitted with wheels to provide a useful trailer when the motorcycle was unpacked and made ready for use. Excelsior started production of the machine in late 1942, with almost 4,000 examples built. The Welbike was deployed during airborne and assault landings at Anzio and Normandy.

Even smaller than the Welbike was the Volugrafo Aeromoto, a tiny 123cc airborne motorcycle produced in Italy from 1942. A rudimentary seat was provided on top of the fuel tank, and with its rectangular duplex frame, folding seat and handlebars, and 715mm/28in wheelbase, it could hardly be considered to be a "real" motorcycle at all, although it was capable of 50kph/30mph. There was no suspension, and the wheels were twinned, front and rear, to help support the weight of a fully kitted airborne soldier. Less than 2,000 were built and it was also used by the *Wehrmacht*.

The US Army had its own airborne machines, in the form of the Cushman Autoglide 53. Resembling an overgrown child's scooter, with balloon tyres providing its only suspension, it was

ABOVE: **The British Excelsior Welbike was designed to fold, thus allowing it to be stowed into a cylindrical air-drop container. It needed push starting and lacked gears but was a useful mode of transport for airborne troops.**

powered by a 246cc single-cylinder engine. Parachute lifting rings were fitted front and rear, which would suggest that the Americans considered a protective cradle or container to be unnecessary. A total of 4,734 examples were completed over a two-year period and it was classified as "limited standard", but photographs of the machine in action are rare.

Although the French used a licence-built Vespa scooter – the ACMA TAP150 – in the airborne role in the mid-1950s, these machines generally disappeared in the post-war years as the advent of larger transport aircraft made them redundant.

LEFT: **It was not only lightweight motorcycles which could be carried in aircraft. Here, *Fallschirmjäger* load a heavy motorcycle combination into a Junkers Ju52.**

The German *Kettenkraftrad* SdKfz 2

The development of the curious *Kettenkraftrad* SdKfz 2 – more usually shortened to *Kettenkrad* and meaning, simply, "half-track motorcycle" – was originated in 1938, by the German Air Force. It was designed by NSU together with input from the German Defence Ministry Office Group 6

(*Wäffenprüfamt 6*) for Development and Testing of Army Weapons and was intended to be used as a light artillery prime mover for the newly formed paratroop (*Fallschirmjäger*) units. It would typically have been required to tow the 7.5cm *Gebrigskanone* 15/28 gun, 2cm FlaK 30 and 38 anti-aircraft guns, or 3.7cm

ABOVE: **The NSU *Kettenkrad* consisted of the front end of a motorcycle attached to a box-like hull which was carried on a standard German half-track system. It was used as a gun tractor and personnel carrier and had seats for two men facing to the rear.** LEFT: **Perhaps the only successful tracked motorcycle, and despite a heavy maintenance requirement, the *Kettenkrad* is popular with military-vehicle enthusiasts.**

Pak 36 anti-tank gun, all of which were suitable for air-transportation but which were too heavy for man-handling.

The basic design for the *Kettenkrad* was derived from the *Motorkarette* – a four-wheeled/half-tracked load-carrying vehicle that had been designed for the Austrian Army by Heinrich Ernst Kniepkamp. A prolific engineer, by the end of the war Kniepkamp had patented around 50 individual designs covering various aspects of track-laying vehicles.

With the *Kettenkrad*, Kniepkamp effectively took the *Motorkarette* design a stage further by marrying a small, box-like steel hull supported on steel tracks to the front end of a motorcycle. Early prototypes had a motorcycle-type spoked front wheel but, on production models, a steel disc wheel was adopted which was presumably stronger and easier to manufacture. The front forks were originally adapted from those used on the NSU 601 OS(L) motorcycle but they proved unequal to the rigours of off-road performance and, in 1942, were replaced by a wholly new pattern incorporating a hydraulic damper. The reverse gear was also a weak point as well as the differential brakes, the latter tended to become contaminated with oil. The brakes were mechanically operated.

Power came from a centrally mounted 1,488cc Opel four-cylinder petrol engine – taken from the company's Olympia motor car – which was connected to a six-speed gearbox (3F1Rx2) located under the driver's saddle. Although the engine output was a modest 37bhp, the vehicle was capable of a speed of 73kph/45mph on the road, while also offering formidable off-road capabilities.

The track system shared some design principles with the other World War II German half-tracks and, like these, the front wheel also provided the initial steering input, with the differential braking system automatically coming into action once the handlebars were turned beyond a certain angle.

The driver sat in the normal motorcycle position, and there was a transverse rear-facing seat for two behind the engine compartment. A small, amphibious, trailer was also designed for use with the vehicle.

Production started in 1939 at NSU's Neckarsülm factory, with the first vehicles delivered during 1940/41; Stoewer also contributed production from 1943. Once production was underway, a larger vehicle was prototyped which would provide seating for a driver plus five men, enabling it to also act as a personnel carrier; the extended track length required five pairs of wheels as opposed to the four pairs of the standard machine. Powered by either the six-cylinder engine of the Opel Kapitän or a Stump K20 engine, ten prototypes were produced of this so-called HK-102 *Grosses Kettenkraftrad*, but there was no series production.

A total of 8,345 vehicles had been constructed by the end of the war and the vehicle remained in production until 1948, marketed as a light agricultural tractor, with perhaps 500–550 more being produced.

Variants

NSU HK-100 Series

SdKfz 2	Half-track, motorcycle, 1/2 ton, tractor; HK-100, HK-101
SdKfz 2	Half-track, motorcycle, 1/2 ton, crane; HK-101
SdKfz 2/1	Half-track, motorcycle, 1/2 ton, field telephone cable layer; HK-101
SdKfz 2/2	Half-track, motorcycle, 1/2 ton, heavy field telephone cable layer; HK-101

ABOVE: **The combination of tracks at the rear, and a high power-to-weight ratio gave the machine a formidable off-road performance.**

Motor tricycles

Tricycles, and even quadricycle machines, were relatively common in the very early years before the motorcycle evolved into its definitive form. Indeed, the British Army had toyed with the AC Auto Carrier tricycle back around the turn of the century. However, the tricycle had disappeared by about 1910 and it was not until the early 1930s that such machines started to reappear. Indian and Harley-Davidson produced motor tricycles in 1932 and 1933 respectively and both machines were provided with a special towbar to provide a convenient means for the automotive service

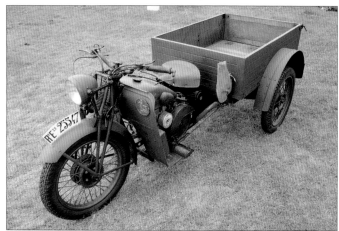

TOP AND ABOVE: **During the late 1930s and in World War II, Italian motorcycle manufacturers produced three-wheeled versions of standard machines. The Moto-Guzzi** *Trialce* **was typical of the type.** LEFT: **Wrecked Japanese** *Sanrinsha* **motor tricycle, probably produced by Kurogane.**

station to collect and deliver customers' cars without requiring a second driver. Harley-Davidson named theirs Servi-Car, Indian chose the name Dispatch-Tow and, although a handful of Servi-Cars entered military service, neither machine was procured in any quantity.

In Italy and Japan it was a different story and the motorized tricycle was commonly used as a commercial load carrier. Both countries produced military versions of the standard civilian machines for use during World War II.

In 1932, Moto-Guzzi introduced a tricycle version of the company's GT17 motorcycle known as the *Mototriciclo Militare 32*. Typical of the design of such machines, a motorcycle front end, in this case with a front fork assembly which incorporated both compression and rebound springs, was married to a rear sub-frame mounting a two-wheeled driven axle. Power was provided by the same 500cc engine as was used for the

ABOVE AND LEFT: **The Indian Motocycle Company produced this tricycle for the US Army in 1940, based on the Chief model; a total of just 16 was purchased.**

motorcycle driving the axle through a four-speed gearbox and exposed chain, but the gear ratios would almost certainly have been reduced to handle the increased weight. The standard body was an open load-carrying box, with a 500kg/1,102lb payload, but there were also fighting variants which mounted a machine-gun in the rear. When the GT17 was replaced by the *Alce*, the three-wheeled variant was known as the *Trialce*, and in 1942, a centre-folding variant was produced called the *Smontabile*. The heavier Moto-Guzzi 500U (*Unificato*) of 1942 was similar but was capable of carrying 1,000kg/1,100lb.

Benelli produced a similar device based on their 500cc motorcycle in 1942. As well as being used as a general load carrier, it was also employed as a communications vehicle and as a tractor for the Italian 47mm anti-tank gun.

Between 1943 and 1963, Gilera also supplied their 500cc *Mercurio* heavy motor tricycle to the Italian Army. Shaft-driven, and with a payload of 1,300kg/2,850lb, this was the largest machine of its type, and was produced with both drop-side cargo and tipper bodies.

The pinnacle of the development of three-wheeled load carriers was probably the Moto-Guzzi *Mulo Meccanico*, a hybrid motorcycle-derived 3x3 load carrier designed in 1959/60. With demountable tracks for the rear wheels, user-adjustable rear axle width, six-speed gearbox, and lockable differentials, it was perfect for the narrow passes of the Italian Alps.

Alongside many others, the Japanese Kurogane company supplied a 3x2 motor tricycle to the Imperial Japanese Army for use both as a personnel carrier and with a 240kg/500lb cargo box. Similar machines were supplied by other companies including Iwasaki and Toyo Kogyo.

The US Army trialled experimental motor tricycles produced by GM-Delco, Harley-Davidson, Indian, and Crosley between 1938 and 1940 but the development of the Jeep appears to have brought these developments to an end. However, the US Army did purchase small numbers of load-carrying three-wheeled scooters for use around bases during World War II. The most numerous of these was the Cushman Model 39 Package Kar, but the Custer light delivery vehicle was similar.

Unlike the Italian and Japanese tricycles, these machines both had a rear-mounted engine driving and steering through a single rear wheel, while the load-carrying box was fitted at the front, supported on a pair of small wheels.

Subsequent lightweight load carriers, including devices such as the DAF Pony which evolved into the the US Army's Mechanical Mule, the British Hunting-Percival Harrier, and of course, recent quad bikes, have tended to be four wheelers.

ABOVE: **Dating from 1959, the Moto-Guzzi *Mulo Meccanico* was probably the pinnacle of motor tricycle design. Powered by a 745cc V-twin engine, it featured drive to all three wheels, extensible rear track and could be fitted with a track system over the rear wheels.**

The Jeep enters service

In 1940, Harley-Davidson produced 15 pre-production examples of what was described as a "field car" for the US Army. The three-seat machine employed the front end of a motorcycle and was clearly derived from Harley's GA Servi-Car, although the rear locker was replaced by a rear-facing bench seat. It was powered by the company's 999cc "knucklehead" engine driving the rear wheels through a three-speed gearbox and propeller shaft. Apparently lacking sufficient power during trials, one of these machines was modified by boring the engine out to 1,130cc.

The trials came to naught and the field car disappeared, little more than a margin note in the development of the military motorcycle. Had it entered production, the little field car might have served in the same kind of roles as the German-built Zündapp and BMW 3x2 motorcycle outfits. In the light of other events taking place in 1940, it is not difficult to understand why this did not happen.

On June 14, 1940, William F. Beasley, Chief Engineer of the US Ordnance Department, drew up the basic requirements for what was to become the Jeep. His free-hand sketch showed a small four-wheeled utility vehicle with cut-away door openings, open sides, a canvas top, and a machine-gun mount. In mid-July, 135 US motor manufacturers were approached to bid for the development and eventual production of this machine –

TOP: **Jeeps were light enough to be carried by glider and were more versatile than the motorcycle.** ABOVE RIGHT: **When the Jeep appeared in 1941, it was used for most of the roles which had previously been assigned to the motorcycle.** RIGHT: **A superbly restored World War II Jeep finished in Royal Airforce markings, displayed at the War and Peace Show, Beltring, Kent.**

LEFT: **The large American motorcycle, typified here by the Harley-Davidson WLA, cost the US Government an average of $380 – although a Jeep cost around $1,000 it was a far more useful vehicle.** BELOW: **Almost 650,000 Jeeps were produced during World War II, and was used by all of the Allies in every theatre of operation. By comparison, Britain and the USA produced something like 550,000 motorcycles during the same period.**

just two responded. American Bantam had a prototype running by September 23. Willys-Overland was a little slower, their prototype, based partly on the work done by Bantam, being delivered to Camp Holabird, Maryland, on November 13. The mighty Ford Motor Company, having been coerced, submitted a prototype ten days later.

Each of the three companies received a contract to construct 1,500 examples of their particular take on Beasley's vehicle. With the manufacturing work underway, elements of the Willys and Ford vehicles were combined to produce a standardized design. Bantam received no more contracts and Willys and Ford built some 640,000 examples of the standardized Jeep between 1941 and 1945.

At 1,575mm/62in, the Jeep was just 254mm/10in wider than Harley's field car. Granted, it weighed almost twice as much – 1,115kg/2,460lb against some 635kg/1,400lb – but it was still light enough to be man-handled when necessary and, it had room for four men, could mount a machine gun or anti-tank rifle, carry stretchers and tow a field gun. But perhaps most importantly, it had four-wheel drive and could go almost anywhere that a tracked vehicle – or a motorcycle – could go.

The Jeep spelled the end of the field car project. It also brought a fundamental change to the way that the US Army – and to some extent, all of the Allies – used the motorcycle. It would be fair to say that from about mid-1942, motorcycles were largely superseded by the ubiquitous Jeep. For example, US Army standing orders had initially decreed that motorcycles be attached to each armoured division, but this practice came to an end in March 1942 when the vehicle type was removed from the Tables of Organization and Equipment (TOE), having been replaced by the Jeep. Of course, this does not mean that armoured units did not use motorcycles; it simply means they were not authorized. Similarly, motorcycles were not listed for

US Army field Military Police (MP) units for the years 1943–45, although camp and station MP units were authorized a maximum of 16 motorcycles – or Jeeps.

The motorcycle remained useful in the airborne role, and for despatch riders, traffic control and convoy escort work but it was never used by the Allies as a combat vehicle in the way that the Germans used their big Zündapp and BMW machines.

The Jeep also effectively ended any further development of the specialized military motorcycle. In the immediate post-war years, the Allies continued to use wartime machines in a restricted range of roles and, when new machines were eventually procured, they were invariably of civilian origin.

Willys did not know how right they were when they coined the slogan, "The sun never sets on the mighty Jeep".

Reaping the whirlwind

During the early years of World War II, German bombers conducted a campaign of attrition against Britain's manufacturing capabilities. Factories, docks and ports were all considered legitimate targets and the strategic bombing carried out by the *Luftwaffe* between September 1940 and May 1941 took its toll on major manufacturing

ABOVE: **The city of Coventry was devastated by German air raids during the night of November 14, 1940. The Triumph motorcycle factory was all but totally destroyed.** BELOW: **During the later years of the war, the Allies exploited their air superiority to hit back at the German war machine.**

centres, particularly in London and the West Midlands. Between November 1940 and February 1941, the campaign was widened to include other important industrial and port cities including Coventry, Southampton, Birmingham, Liverpool, Bristol, Swindon, Plymouth, Cardiff, Manchester, Sheffield, Portsmouth and Avonmouth (Bristol).

The German bombing raids spelled disaster for many companies who were never able to recover from the loss of plant, tools and equipment.

One of the worst raids of 1940 took place on the night of November 14 when the *Luftwaffe* devastated the West Midlands city of Coventry. The *Luftwaffe* was using a new navigation technique called *X-Gerät* in which a radio beam led the pathfinder squadron *Kampfgeschwader 100* to the target. The job of the pathfinders was to drop incendiary bombs which would start fires, these, in turn, guiding the bombers of *Luftflotte 3*. More than 500 bombers took part in the raid, dropping 30,000 incendiary bombs and 500 tons of high explosive on the city. Reports later estimated that 4,330 homes were destroyed and 75 per cent of the city's factories were affected.

Coventry was home to Daimler, Armstrong Whitworth, Courtaulds, GEC, Dunlop, Alvis, and of course Triumph motorcycles. Triumph's Priory Street works was so badly damaged that the company was forced to move production to a temporary location in Warwick, while a new factory on the Birmingham–Coventry road outside Meriden was built. Staff salvaged what they could from the ruins, including tools and usable parts, but the first batch of 50 3TW "twins" was destroyed, effectively bringing this model to an untimely end and, although Triumph struggled on in what remained usable at the Priory Street works, it was not really until June 1941 that full-scale production resumed. The bombing also destroyed all of Triumph's technical records, drawings and designs.

Less than a week later, on November 19, 1940, BSA's Small Heath factory was also directly hit by German bombers. A large section of the original 1915 workshop in Armoury Road was destroyed, killing 53 nightshift workers. Two nights later, a second raid almost completely destroyed the old 1863 structure. BSA lost 1,600 machine tools in these two raids, badly affecting the company's manufacturing ability.

However, by 1944, the tide had turned and strategic bombing action by the RAF and the USAF was systematically destroying Germany's industrial base. The German tank, truck and armaments industries became primary targets and, while motorcycle plants were not deliberately attacked, the bombing forced many factories to be relocated. At this stage in the war, there was no possibility of constructing new facilities and the only way to continue with production was for the manufacturers who were within range of the Allied bombers to disperse undamaged machines and production lines to existing sites elsewhere. This had the effect of displacing other activities that were taking place. For example, BMW was forced to turn over most of its München plant to producing aircraft engines, effectively ending motorcycle production there. Both NSU and Zündapp, with plants located in Neckarsulm and Stuttgart respectively, also reduced the number of motorcycles produced in order to concentrate on other armaments. In Austria, Steyr ceased the production of motorcycles in favour of trucks. Other plants were unable to continue as a direct result of Allied action – the Ardie plant at Nürnberg was destroyed, as was the small engine producing plant of Fichtel & Sachs at Hamburg.

By 1944, the effects of the bombing raids combined with a savage standardization programme of military motor vehicles meant that Auto-Union DKW had become the only German motorcycle manufacturer producing any volume. The company's Zschopau factory continued to produce 125cc and 350cc machines for as long as the raw materials were available but, by March 1945, the shortages were so acute that all motor vehicle production in Germany effectively came to an end. How the mighty had fallen – in 1939, German motorcycle production had topped 200,000 units. By 1944 the effects of bombing, shortages of materials and components, and plant dispersal had reduced this figure to little more than 30,000.

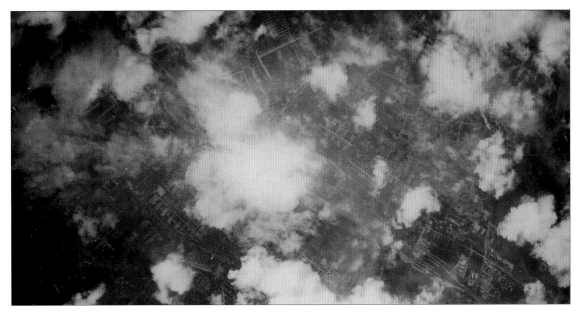

ABOVE AND LEFT: **The Allies used a target prioritization system to attack German centres of production, often forcing factories to relocate. Motorcycle factories were not specifically targeted but, by the end of the war, the Ardie plant had been destroyed. DKW was the only motorcycle manufacturer to remain in production.**

Military motorcycles in France

The French Army started buying trucks and motorcars and, in smaller quantities, motorcycles before the turn of the 19th century. Peugeot, René Gillet, and Werner had all started producing motorcycles in France before 1900, followed by Terrot and Griffon in 1901 and 1902, respectively. Although Terrot grew to become the largest motorcycle manufacturer in France, and supplied large numbers of machines to the French Army, the domestic industry was not generally ever able to meet the demand for military motorcycles.

Werner closed in 1908, and most of the French motorcycles deployed during World War I and in the inter-war years, came from Terrot and René Gillet, both of them having acquired a reputation for producing reliable, robust machines. The René Gillet machine of 1916 was often fitted with an ambulance or machine-gun sidecar.

ABOVE: **French motorcycle outriders accompany a Panhard-powered Citroën-Kégresse half-track armoured car of 1929. The exposed flywheel of the lead motorcycle suggests a Motobécane B4 or B44 of the early 1930s.**

Mechanization continued slowly in the immediate post-war years, but the French Army continued to purchase motorcycles from the domestic suppliers, albeit in small numbers. The products of René Gillet and Terrot continued to feature heavily and although Griffon had closed in the late 1920s, new manufacturers, such as Gnome & Rhône (1919), Motobécane (1923) and Monet Goyon (1917), had also been established.

The 750cc René Gillet Model G, introduced in 1926, and the later G1, was among the most widely used, for both solo and specialized sidecar work, right up until the outbreak of World War II. Newcomers Gnome & Rhône produced two heavy machines that were widely used by the French as well as

ABOVE: **Monet-Goyon's L5 model, and the subsequent L5A1, was a standard production machine widely used in solo and sidecar form by the French Army and the *Gendarmerie* (police).** LEFT: **The French company Monet-Goyon produced high-quality motorcycles in the British style between 1917 and 1957.**

being requisitioned by, and perhaps even produced for, the *Wehrmacht* after 1940. The first of these was the 750cc *Armée* of 1935, but in 1938 this was replaced by the 800cc AX2 which featured shaft drive, four-speed forward and reverse gearbox, and driven sidecar wheel. Gnome & Rhône's 500cc D5A was also widely used, as was the Terrot 500cc RDA, both machines dating from 1938.

The Simca-SEVITAME Type B *Armée* of 1938/39 – the acronym stands for *Société d'Etude des Véhicules Issus de la Technique Automobile Moderne et Economique* – is worth describing if only for its technical innovation. Designed by Marcel Violet, the engine was a 330cc in-line twin-cylinder unit installed with the crankshaft at the top and the cylinders facing down; cooling was achieved by means of some 12 litres/2.65 gallons of oil. Final drive was by exposed shaft and a small propeller could be attached to the shaft to allow the motorcycle to be used as an outboard to power a boat. The fuel tank formed the rear mudguard. Few had been manufactured by the time France fell to Germany in 1940.

Sadly the domestic motorcycle industry remained unable to supply the Army's needs even up to World War II, and, in 1939, the French Army had ordered 5,000 Indian Chiefs from the USA. Although the machines had been manufactured by March 1940, the fall of France in May meant that there was not sufficient time to make delivery and the machines were diverted to Britain. Similarly, a number of motorcycles ordered from Ariel and Velocette during 1939/40 were also diverted to the British Army.

The French motorcycle industry never really recovered from World War II. René Gillet closed in 1957 as did Koehler

ABOVE: **At one time, Terrot was the largest motorcycle manufacturer in France, and the company's 500cc RDA, dating from 1938, was typical of the larger French motorcycles of the pre-war period. The factory's Dijon location put it out of reach of the occupying Germans but production was halted in 1944.**

and Monet-Goyon; Gnome & Rhône survived until 1959 and Terrot staggered on against falling sales until the early 1960s. Only Peugeot has survived to the present day.

As with most Western armies, the military motorcycle fell from favour during the 1960s but, during the previous decade the French Army had procured various domestic machines, including the 170cc Peugeot 176TC4 and the earlier 176D4, the 200cc Gnome & Rhône LX200, and the 500cc Terrot RGST. By 1960, with very little domestic motorcycle industry remaining, the government purchased a number of 250cc BMW R-27TS machines, followed, in 1966, by the Triumph T20WD, a derivative of the Tiger Cub. In 1978, the tiny Peugeot SX8 and SX8T *Armée* was procured for off-road use, and although it saw 20 years of service, it was always felt to lack sufficient power.

LEFT: **Belgian Army motorcycle troops with radio equipped sidecars. In the late 1930s, the Belgian manufacturers FN, Sarolea and Gillet-Herstal all produced heavy motorcycle combination outfits that included selectable drive to the sidecar wheel.**
BELOW LEFT AND BELOW: **Sarolea produced motorcycles from 1898 to 1957, including many military machines. This is the side-valve AS350 dating from 1951; there was a similar 400cc model designated 51-A4.**

Military motorcycles in Belgium

During the first three or four decades of motorcycling, more than 100 factories had been established in Belgium but by the time the Belgian Army started mechanization in the 1930s, it seems that only a handful of these manufacturers remained in business. The three that were chosen to supply military motorcycles were all based in the Liège town of Herstal, some 65km/40 miles east of Brussels. The Sarolea company had established a workshop in the town in 1898, and was almost certainly the first Belgian motorcycle manufacturer. FN followed in 1901, becoming

known for its use of shaft drive from 1903. Gillet-Herstal had started producing motorcycles in 1919, and was presumably so-named to differentiate it from the French René Gillet concern, which had been established in business some 20 years earlier.

Small numbers of basically civilian FN motorcycles were used by the Belgian Army before and during World War I, and a number of the company's 2.75hp machines were used by the Australian Army. It was not until the 1930s that the country started seriously mechanizing its army and, from 1935/36

onwards, Gillet-Herstal, Sarolea and FN machines were purchased for the Belgian Army, with numbers of the latter also supplied to the Soviet and Swiss armies.

There was nothing remarkable about the majority of Belgian motorcycles but in the mid-1930s, in response to a requirement for a heavy motorcycle capable of operating in all types of ground conditions, all three Belgian manufacturers started to produce specialized military sidecar outfits with sidecar-wheel drive, high ground clearance and reverse gear.

Dating from 1937, the FN M12-SM was the first of these to be taken into service. It was a big, heavy-duty machine powered by a 1,000cc horizontally opposed side-valve engine driving the rear wheel and the sidecar wheel through a four-speed forward and reverse gearbox together with a two-speed transfer case. The same year, Sarolea produced the 600cc single-cylinder S6, following this in 1939 with the horizontally opposed H1000 *Militaire*, the latter equipped with a three-speed forward and reverse gearbox and two-speed transfer case. Gillet-Herstal produced their 750 in 1938, powered by a vertical twin engine and also featuring sidecar-wheel drive and a four-speed forward and reverse gearbox, although this time lacking the low-ratio gears of the transfer case. A motor tricycle was also produced, based on the FN M12-SM, between 1939 and 1940.

These unique Belgian machines, which pre-date the big Zündapp and BMW 3x2 sidecar outfits, were both captured and copied by the *Wehrmacht*, and were also supplied to many other countries including Argentina, Chile, China and the Middle East.

Although motorcycle production in Belgium was certainly seriously curtailed during the war years, all three companies resumed manufacturing motorcycles in the post-war period. Sarolea had formed a co-operative with a number of other Belgian manufacturers, including Gillet-Herstal, and generally

ABOVE AND BELOW: **Dating from 1947, the single-cylinder FN M13 was typical of medium motorcycles of the period. Although it was fitted with front suspension, the rear end remained unsprung. A selection of engines was available, including 250cc, 350cc and 450cc units.**

concentrated on two-strokes, while FN attempted to regain their market share with a range of 250cc to 500cc models. Both Sarolea and FN stopped making motorcycles in 1957, while Gillet-Herstal managed to survive into the early 1960s.

The Belgian Army used British and American machines in the immediate post-war years including Indian, Harley-Davidson, Ariel, Matchless, and Norton. All three of the domestic manufacturers also supplied small numbers of 350, 400 and 450cc side-valve motorcycles to the Belgian Army during the 1950s. A number of Harley-Davidson FL Electra-Glides were also purchased by the *Rijkwascht* in 1967 for military police duties, possibly the last use of a full-size Harley-Davidson by a European army.

During 1959, FN produced about 500 examples of their three-wheeled AS24 air-portable tricycle that was built under licence from Straussler and could be used as an ambulance, cargo or personnel carrier, fire-fighter or missile launcher.

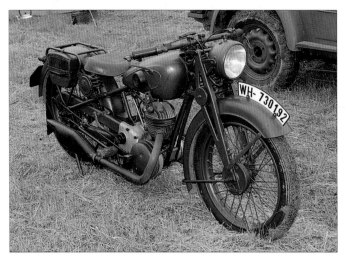

Military motorcycles in Germany

The German Imperial Army was quick to recognize the military potential of the motorcycle. The first such machines were trialled in 1899 and a number were taken into German military service as early as 1904, By 1918, the Germans had procured more than 5,400 motorcycles. Equally, of the main protagonists of World War II, Germany was always the most enthusiastic user of motorcycles – and, for that matter, horses – both of which were used in great numbers by all arms of the service during the early years of the conflict. Alongside the rather more mundane roles such as despatch riding, motorcycles were also employed by the elite and highly mobile combat troops known as *Kradschützen* which formed such an effective part of the lightning Blitzkrieg tactic.

At the end of the 1930s, the *Wehrmacht* had literally dozens of different, mostly civilian style, machines in service and it is said that there was a total of one million motorcycles in military service by 1937. Stockholding of parts was clearly something of a nightmare and, by 1940, the *Wehrmacht* had standardized

on motorcycles in three categories – light, medium and heavy – from a smaller number of manufacturers.

Light motorcycles, with engines under 350cc, were typically produced by BMW, DKW, NSU and TWN (Triumph). The most numerous of such machines was the NSU 251OS(L) of which some 35,000 were produced between 1934 and 1944. Basically a lightly modified commercial motorcycle, it was powered by an overhead valve engine of 241cc, had a top speed of 100kph/62mph, and a range of around 325km/200 miles. The rigid rear forks and parallelogram front suspension were typical of the period.

In the "medium" category, motorcycles were powered by an engine of between 350cc and 500cc and were typically produced by DKW, TWN and Victoria. Motorcycles in the "heavy" category were generally powered by a big 600 to 750cc flat-twin engine; Zündapp even had an 800cc model. These machines were invariably used in conjunction with a standardized military sidecar, often with a driven wheel. Such machines, produced by BMW, NSU, and Zündapp, were used on all fronts as well as in airborne operations, and the BMW R-75 is representative of the type; produced between 1940 and 1944, it was powered by a 746cc horizontally opposed overhead-valve engine driving a rear axle which was shared by the motorcycle and sidecar, and which incorporated a lockable differential. A machine-gun was frequently mounted on the sidecar, which could also carry additional supplies of fuel and ammunition.

In addition, motorcycles produced by the Belgian FN and French Gnome & Rhône companies were also impressed into service, and there were also thousands of requisitioned civilian machines and other captured enemy motorcycles in service.

And, of course, Germany remained unique in employing a half-tracked motorcycle – the SdKfz 2, better known as the NSU HK-101 *Kettenkraftrad* – usually shortened to simply *Kettenkrad*. Offering excellent cross-country performance, it was powered by the 1,488cc engine of the contemporary Opel Olympia motorcar, and could accommodate a crew of three and tow a gun or light trailer.

ABOVE: **Germany used thousands of motorcycles during World War II and not all were of the heavy variety. On the left is a 198cc NSU 201, on the right, a DKW NZ-350, with a capacity of 346cc.** BELOW: **The 340cc single-cylinder BMW R-35, dating from 1937, was widely used as a training machine.**

But a combination of Allied bombing and the increasing demand for all kinds of military equipment meant that Germany struggled to produce sufficient motorcycles for the *Wehrmacht*'s needs. Between 1934 and 1939, the German armed forces took delivery of almost 70,000 motorcycles and, for the years 1940 to 1943, the number rose to 277,000. However, as Germany's factories strained to satisfy the war effort, many motorcycle manufacturers found themselves producing other war materials. By 1943, more than 80 per cent of the production facilities at

ABOVE: **Massed ranks of German motorcycle combinations taking the salute as they drive slowly past the *Führer*.**

the Ardie, Steyr, TWN, Victoria and DKW factories were devoted to producing tank components, stationary engines, arms and ammunition, rather than motorcycles.

Some German motorcycle production had resumed by the late 1940s and, while BMW might be a notable exception, many of the manufacturers never regained their pre-war markets.

ABOVE: **The band of the *Nationalsozialistisches Kraftfahrkorps*, NSKK (National Socialist Motor Corps – an organization of the Nazi Party) in 1937.**
RIGHT: **Lightweight motorcycles, with single-cylinder two-stroke engines of around 100cc, were widely used to provide mobility in the German Army. Typical machines were supplied by Ardie, Phänomen, DKW and TWN (Triumph).**

Military motorcycles in Great Britain

Britain was among the first users of military motorcycles, with motorcycle-mounted despatch riders used for the first time during manoeuvres in 1910. During World War I, the most numerous British Army motorcycles were lightly militarized civilian machines supplied by Triumph and Douglas which had been standardized for military service. Dozens of other, often unsuitable, types were also used, many being impressed civilian machines.

During the 1930s, the War Office attempted to standardize on a 500cc V-twin military motorcycle but, despite trialling dozens of UK and sometimes foreign machines, appeared unable to find anything which was suitable. By the outbreak of World War II, the typical British Army motorcycle was a low-cost single-cylinder machine that could be built in large numbers. Even so, production was not increased at a sufficient rate and in September 1939, some 30 per cent of the British Army's 21,000 motorcycles were impressed civilian types. Then, when the British Expeditionary Force abandoned thousands of its newest motorcycles in France and Belgium following the evacuations from Dunkirk, there was an immediate, and critical shortage of suitable machines. There was a period when anything that could move was purchased for military service, including hundreds of not terribly suitable civilian machines that happened to be in the showrooms or awaiting delivery.

With the immediate crises resolved, it would be fair to say that the typical British military motorcycle of World War II was a thoroughly conventional design, generally derived from a pre-war civilian machine. Most were powered by a 350cc or

TOP RIGHT: **Motorcycle outriders leading a transport convoy through the ruins of a town in Normandy.**
ABOVE RIGHT: **British despatch riders taking a break after the D-Day landings.**
RIGHT: **Introduced in 1939 and remaining in production until 1945, the 500cc side-valve BSA M20 was probably the longest-serving motorcycle in the British Army.**

ABOVE: **Sidecars were not widely used by the British services. This BSA M20 Swallow sidecar combination is marked as belonging to the RAF.** RIGHT: **The Royal Navy also used the M20; the civilian number plate suggests a very early machine.**

500cc single-cylinder side-valve engine driving the rear wheel through a four-speed gearbox and exposed chain; some manufacturers, for example Triumph, managed to graduate from side valves to overhead valves. With perhaps the notable exception of the Matchless G3L which had telescopic forks, front suspension was provided by coil-sprung parallelogram girder forks, while the rear end remained unsprung.

Sidecars were not widely used although the factory-produced Norton 633 Big Four should be mentioned as the only British combination outfit to be fitted with a driven sidecar wheel. At the other end of the scale, the tiny Excelsior Welbike "para-scooter", powered by a 98cc two-stroke engine which drove the rear wheel directly, was designed to be air-dropped in a standard container.

During this period, technical development generally took a back seat to the exigencies of production, often in the face of materials shortages and, occasionally, almost overwhelming *Luftwaffe* action, and a total of 425,000 military motorcycles poured out of Britain's motorcycle factories in the years 1940 to 1945. With the Jeep taking care of many roles for which the motorcycle would have been considered during the 1930s, this was more than enough for the needs of the British and the Commonwealth armies, with more than a few exported to the Soviet Union. Motorcycles were used by the Army, the RAF and the Royal Navy throughout World War II, as well as by the Home Guard and Civil Defence services.

The British manufacturers were quick to get civilian production underway again after the war, albeit with little more than warmed-over versions of pre-war models. The British Army retained the best, and least used, motorcycles from the war years, with the BSA M20 and the Matchless G3L notably remaining in service into the 1950s, but a number of Triumph TRW twins were bought at the end of the 1940s. When new machines were purchased in the 1960s, they were little more than lightly militarized versions of the then current BSA A65 and B40, Matchless G3LS, and the Triumph 500. In the late 1970s, the BSA-assembled Bombardier Can-Am 250 replaced the British

motorcycles and this, in turn, gave way to the Armstrong/Harley-Davidson MT350 and MT500, while powerful Norton police motorcycles were replaced by the Honda Pan-European.

Despite a few World War II experiments with machine-gun equipped sidecars, the British Army did not generally use motorcycles for a combat role, preferring to employ them for despatch riders, convoy escort, traffic control, and military police duties – and, of course, in the Royal Signals "White Helmets" display team that first saw the light of day in 1927.

ABOVE: **The side-valve Triumph 2SW was supplied to the War Office between 1938 and 1941, with more than 10,000 examples built.**

Military motorcycles in the Commonwealth

During World War I, Canadian and Australian forces were equipped with a similar range of machines as the British Army, notably the Douglas 2.75hp, BSA Model H, and Triumph Model H. It was much the same story for World War II, and although the industries of Canada, Australia, New Zealand, India and South Africa all constructed military vehicles during World War II, none of these nations produced military motorcycles. With but a single exception, there were no domestic motorcycle manufacturers in the Commonwealth and the armies generally operated motorcycles which had been manufactured in either Britain or the USA.

That exception was Australia, where there was a single domestic motorcycle, the lightweight Villiers-powered Waratah produced by Williams Brothers of Sydney who were in business from 1914 to 1948, but none appear to have been supplied to the Australian services. In Canada, Bombardier did not start producing motorcycles until 1973 and Royal Enfield did not establish their factory in India until 1955. Hence, all Commonwealth military motorcycles of World War II came from overseas.

The Canadian Army Vehicle Data Book, issued by Canadian Military Headquarters in March 1944, lists just three motorcycles: two from Britain – the Matchless G3L and the Norton 16H, both of which were classed as "light", and the US-built Harley-Davidson WLC, which was described as "heavy". However, the Canadians almost certainly also used Indian 340 and 640 machines and Harley-Davidson WLAs.

The Harley-Davidson WLC was developed especially for the Canadian Department of National Defense, and was introduced

in 1941. It is the closest thing there is to a Canadian military motorcycle and was produced in what were described as "domestic" and "export" models, both incorporating a number of detailed changes when compared to the standard US Army WLA. These changes included British-style right-hand clutch-

ABOVE LEFT: **Canadian forces made use of the British BSA M20.** ABOVE: **South African Army Commandos mounted on Harley-Davidsons.** BELOW: **The machine nearest the camera is a Matchless G3 with a decidedly flat rear tyre.**

LEFT: **The ubiquitous BSA M20 was as popular with Commonwealth units as it was with British. These new machines, costing £49.50 each, were part of a contract for 4,000 dating from 1940.**
BELOW: **South African women riders on civilian machines; the motorcycle nearest the camera is a Royal Enfield, probably a Model C from which the WD/C was derived.**

ABOVE: **A Canadian despatch rider on a Norton 16H consults his rotating map while on exercise in England in 1943.**

and-throttle configuration, with the ignition-timing lever also on the right, and different lighting arrangements, which tended to reflect British military practice. There was also a different instrument nacelle, slightly smaller mudguards, and an ammunition/spare parts box carried on the front mudguard; the WLC did not carry the rifle scabbard or ammunition box of the US Army machines. A number of WLCs were fitted with a Goulding single-seat sidecar, in which form it may have been described as Model WLS.

Although the WLA remained in volume production to 1945, and even beyond, the WLC was discontinued in 1944 after 5,356 examples had been built.

As regards machines of British origin, BSA had been supplying motorcycles to both India and South Africa during 1938/39 and, of course, many of these machines remained in service during the war. After 1940, the armies of all of the Commonwealth countries were reinforced with equipment from Britain, including for example Matchless G3L, BSA M20, and Norton 16H motorcycles. Harley-Davidson, and Indian machines were also supplied under the Lend-Lease arrangements, in both solo and sidecar combination form as appropriate. It is also worth noting that in 1942/43 South Africa uniquely received 1,597 examples of the Harley-Davidson Model US sidecar outfit, fitted with a left-hand LLE sidecar, and supplied through the British Supply Council.

Many of these wartime machines remained in service well into the 1950s, the BSA M20 and Matchless G3L proving to have particular longevity. Australia, Canada, India and Pakistan, and South Africa all continued to buy British military motorcycles, the Triumph TRW and BSA B40 being particularly popular.

Military motorcycles in the USA

In 1900, Columbia was the first company to offer a proper motorcycle for sale in the United States. By the following year, there were more than a dozen competitors, including the Indian machine designed by George M. Hendee and Oscar Hedstrom; Harley-Davidson was established in 1904. During the early years of the industry, the US motorcycles differed from their European counterparts in using sturdier frames and well-sprung saddles as a response to the generally poor roads, and in being fitted with better lighting and braking equipment. By the end of the 20th century, the USA had been home to some 325 manufacturers of motorcycles. Hendee had initially laid claim to being the largest motorcycle manufacturer in the world, with sales growing from just 143 in 1902 to 20,000 in 1912, but the title soon passed to Harley-Davidson.

Harley-Davidson was probably the first US motorcycle manufacturer to supply machines to the military, having supplied the Japanese Imperial Army back in 1912. The US Army started buying motorcycles from Hendee (Indian) in 1913, with Harley-Davidsons following in 1916. During World War I, Indian, Harley-Davidson, Excelsior and Cleveland motorcycles were all supplied to the US Expeditionary Force as well as to the Western Allies. The machines were generally used by scouts and despatch riders but, as in Europe, there were also experiments with using sidecars as a stretcher carrier or machine-gun mount.

However, the appearance of cheap motorcars had a profound effect on the growth of the US motorcycle industry, with many pioneering companies forced into early bankruptcy. Cyclone, Thor, Pope, Yale, Iver Johnson and Peerless all closed before

ABOVE: **The iconic Harley-Davidson WLA was the most common US military motorcycle of World War II. A Dodge WC52 weapons carrier provides the backdrop.**
LEFT: **Derived from Harley-Davidson's civilian Model WL, something like 78,000 WLAs were produced between March 1940 and May 1945.**

ABOVE: **A US soldier of the 315th Engineer Battalion, 90th Infantry Division carries everything he needs for his daily routine on his Harley WLA.**

the end of World War I, with Indian, Cleveland, Harley-Davidson and Excelsior – who had absorbed Henderson – being the only significant companies to survive into the 1920s. Cleveland failed in 1929 and when Henderson and Excelsior closed in 1931 only Harley-Davidson and Indian survived – the Hendee company having finally changed its name in 1923.

During World War II, the two surviving volume producers supplied the majority of the motorcycles used by the US Army, as well as supplying machines to Britain, the British Commonwealth, China and the Soviet Union. The military products of both companies were derived from pre-war civilian models although both also developed sidecar combination machines with a driven wheel in the style of the big German BMW and Zündapp motorcycles. By the time the machines were deemed ready for production, events had overcome them and the need had passed, with no series production being commissioned. Small

numbers of specialized motorcycles were also supplied by Cushman and Simplex, with tiny motorized package delivery vehicles coming from Salsbury and Strimple.

In the early days of World War II, motorcycles were widely held by US armoured and infantry combat units and were used for scouting and reconnaissance duties as well being considered a form of mechanized cavalry. The appearance of the Jeep put paid to this and after 1942, the role of the military motorcycle was downgraded and the machines were generally reserved for military police, traffic and convoy control, and despatch riding.

Both Indian and Harley-Davidson resumed civilian production in 1945 but Indian finally closed the doors in 1953, leaving Harley-Davidson as the only volume domestic motorcycle manufacturer. The company generally eschewed the lightweight end of the market and concentrated on the traditional heavy American motorcycle.

Sales continued to the US and other armies during the 1950s and 1960s but the numbers were not significant and it was not until 1987 that Harley-Davidson became, albeit briefly, a significant player in the military market again when the company purchased the rights to the British Armstrong MT350 and MT500. Hoping to secure a big US Army contract, they continued to manufacture the Rotax-engined MT, using parts from all over the world, and to supply the British and Canadian armies who had been buying from Armstrong. A number of MT500s were also used by USAF "combat control teams" but the big US order never materialized, the US Army going on to buy the Kawasaki KL-250D8. Total production of all MT models, by Armstrong and Harley-Davidson during a near 20-year production run was 4,470 units.

The US Army has been one of the prime developers in the RMCS/HDT diesel motorcycle project and continues to operate motorcycles although these days they are far more likely to be of Japanese manufacture.

BELOW LEFT: **The 1,213cc Harley-Davidson Model U was produced between 1937 and 1948, with more than 33,000 examples built, with several thousand of these supplied to the US Government for both sidecar and solo use.** BELOW: **The Cushman Package Kar.**

ABOVE: **The Bianchi 500M was unusual for the time in having plunger-type rear suspension.** LEFT: **Introduced in 1939, some 7,000 examples of the Moto-Guzzi 500cc *Alce* were produced during World War II.**

Military motorcycles in Italy

The Italian Army started mechanization by purchasing a single Fiat motorcar in 1903; motorcycles followed, in small numbers, from 1914 with essentially civilian machines coming from manufacturers such as Bianchi, Frera and Gilera. Of these, Bianchi, which had been established in 1897, was almost certainly the first motorcycle manufacturer in Italy, with Frera established in 1906 and Gilera in 1909.

During World War I, the belt-drive 500cc Bianchi Type A was probably the most numerous motorcycle in use with the Italian Army, but the 570cc and 795cc Frera machines were also widely employed, in both solo and combination form. By 1918, the Italian Army had almost 6,500 motorcycles in service, all of them being lightly militarized commercial models. Few purchases were made in the post-war years and many of the older machines remained in service into the early 1920s. Following the coming to power of Benito Mussolini in 1922, efforts were made to reorganize the Italian motorcycle industry and the army started buying motorcycles again from the early 1930s. The Moto-Guzzi *Militare* 32 motor tricycle was adopted by the army for a range of roles from 1932, including artillery tractor, cargo and personnel carrier, and as a gun platform.

The Benelli company, which had been established in 1917 to supply engines to other manufacturers, started producing motorcycles in 1921 and from the mid-1930s the company

became one of the big three suppliers to the Italian Army, alongside Moto-Guzzi and Gilera. For a number of years during the late 1930s, the Italian Army attempted to develop armoured motorcycles which could be used by snipers. One of these, based on the Moto-Guzzi GT17 could be fitted with armoured leg shields and a screen through which the rider was expected to aim and fire a light machine-gun but like all such efforts elsewhere, it was eventually abandoned as being top heavy and impractical.

Bianchi, Moto-Guzzi, Gilera and Sertum all produced specialized military motorcycles during World War II, with motor tricycles also coming from the first three named companies as well as Benelli. Volugrafo, a company which appears only to have operated during the war years, but which is notable for being the manufacturer of the first modern motor scooter, produced a very small air-portable machine for military use, which was derived from its scooter.

In the years immediately following World War II, the Italian motorcycle industry was quick to re-establish itself, with the Moto-Guzzi *Superalce* and the Gilera *Saturno* both launched in 1946. Both of these models, as well as the Gilera 175GT (1956) were widely used by the Italian Army. Benelli began production a little later, having had its factory destroyed. The company's first post-war machine was not launched until 1949 by which time it appears to have been too late to procure further military contracts.

The 1959 Moto-Guzzi *Mulo Meccanico* should also be mentioned as an all-terrain successor to the motor tricycles of the 1930s. With its 750cc V-twin engine, torque-dividing differential and 3x3 driveline, together with operator controls to reduce the rear tracks on the move, and the ability to be fitted with tracks on the rear wheels, it was far more capable than

LEFT: **First produced in 1942, the Moto-Guzzi 500U *Unificato* is a typical Italian *Motocarro* of the period.**

its predecessors and 200 units were supplied to the Alpine Regiment for use on mountain tracks and passes. In a similar vein, MV Augusta also built the German Faun *Kraka* under licence although, as a four-wheeled vehicle with a conventional steering wheel, this machine is outside the scope of this book.

During the 1960s, Moto-Guzzi made a name for itself as a producer of high-quality powerful motorcycles which might be considered as an alternative to the big BMWs and its 500–950cc machines were widely used in Italy and elsewhere, the V7 and the *Nuovo Falcone*, both dating from 1967, being particular favourites for convoy escort and military police duties. These machines were followed by the 850-T3 and the semi-automatic V1000 *Convert*, dating from 1973 and 1975, respectively.

Unique among European motorcycle industries, Italy seems to have survived the Japanese "invasion" with Benelli, Gilera and Moto-Guzzi all intact, and has even managed to find export orders for its military machines.

TOP AND ABOVE: **Moto-Guzzi retained the horizontal single-cylinder engine (installed along the axis of the machine) together with the exposed flywheel into the post-war years. This is the 500cc *Falcone*, introduced in 1966.** LEFT: **British riders on captured Italian machines, probably Gileras.**

Military motorcycles in the USSR

During World War I, the Russian Imperial Army used motorcycles supplied by, for example, Clyno, Sunbeam and Rudge in Britain, as well as others. Some efforts were made in the mid-1920s to design a heavy military motorcycle in the Soviet Union but these came to nothing and the earliest domestic machine in Soviet military service was probably the IZH-7 (L300) of 1933, a 293cc solo motorcycle produced by the Izhevsk Steel Plant (ISH). Other models followed from the same plant including the prototypes for the purpose-designed military motorcycle combination which subsequently entered production as the PMZ NATI A-750.

The PMZ NATI A-750 featured a mix of Indian and BMW design features and went into production in 1935, until it was eventually replaced by the M-72 in 1939. Between 1936 and 1943, the Tagnarog plant also produced the TIM-AM600 (sometimes identified as TIZ-AM600).

ABOVE RIGHT: **During World War II, the Soviet Union used large numbers of US and British motorcycles to supplement their own production.**
RIGHT: **The Red Army has always been an enthusiastic user of the military motorcycle, with more than 1.5 million machines taken into service over a 90-year period.** BELOW: **The Soviet M-72 was based heavily on the pre-war BMW R-71.**

The best-known Soviet military motorcycle is almost certainly the M-72, which was first produced in 1942, and was used in both solo and sidecar configuration. Based heavily on a pre-war BMW, probably the R-71 since this had been produced under licence in the Soviet Union in 1938, it was powered by a 750cc horizontally opposed side-valve engine and featured shaft drive to the rear wheel via a four-speed gearbox. The original Soviet plan was that the machine would be produced at factories in Moscow, Leningrad (now Saint Petersburg), and Kharkov. The imminent threat of German bombing and subsequent invasion led to the removal of the Moscow facilities to Irbit (the factory being known as IMZ, or Irbit Moto Zavod), and the Leningrad and Kharkov facilities to Gorkiy Moto Zavod (GMZ). During World War II, a total of 9,799 M-72 motorcycles were built and delivered to the Red Army.

In 1949, the M-72 production line was moved again, this time from Gorkiy, (now called Nizhny Novgorod) to the Kiev Motor Zavod (KMZ) in Ukraine, which had been established in 1946. By 1950, 30,000 machines had been produced.

LEFT: **The spirit of the M-72 lives on through various machines – this is the Dniepr M-12 of 1977, which retains the horizontally opposed side-valve engine.** BELOW: **The Mayday parades have always been used as a means of demonstrating the military might of the Soviet Union; these machine-gun equipped infantrymen are riding TIM (TIZ) AM600 solo machines.**

In various forms, and under names which have included Cossack, Ural and, from 1967, Dniepr, the M-72 has remained in almost continuous production. The original M-72 was produced until around 1956; subsequent variants were designated M-72K, M-72H and finally M-72M, with production finally ending in 1960. A civilian model was produced from 1954 by IMZ under the designation K-750. The Chinese motorcycle manufacturer, Chang Jiang, eventually bought the production line for the Ural M-72 to build its CJ-750 motorcycle.

The purely military MV-750, introduced in 1964, featured a power-sharing differential which allowed the rider to choose to feed equal power to the sidecar and motorcycle wheels or 67 per cent of the power to the rear wheel of the motorcycle, and 33 per cent to the sidecar.

The civilian K-750 provided the basis for the Dniepr MT-12 model of 1977, a 750cc heavy motorcycle for sidecar use, still retaining side valves, and fitted with a four-speed forward and reverse gearbox. Later models, such as the MT-9 and MT-10, used an overhead-valve engine.

More than 1.5 million motorcycles have been constructed for use by the Red Army to date, and motorcycle production continues at the Kiev KMZ plant today, with the MT-11 and MT-16. Of course, the former Soviet Socialist Republic of Ukraine has been an independent state since 1990.

The Dniepr 750 machine was used for presidential escort work during the Soviet period and continues to be favoured by President Vladimir Putin. Soviet airborne forces continue to deploy lightweight motorcycles, using them at checkpoints and to control traffic and check dispersed communications installations. Current Soviet thinking has also seen motorcycle combinations armed with heavy machine-guns, and trials have also been conducted mounting anti-tank guided weapons on motorcycle sidecar chassis.

Military motorcycles in Japan

Although it should be pointed out that the Japanese Army has never been a great user of military motorcycles, no-one could argue that the Japanese motorcycle industry does not dominate the world. But it was not always thus and it would seem that the country did not actually start building motorcycles until 1932.

However, the first military use of motorcycles in Japan had begun in 1912 when Harley-Davidson had supplied a number of machines "without spares" to the Japanese Imperial Army for evaluation – almost certainly 492cc single-cylinder

Model X-8-A civilian machines. Japan's involvement in World War I brought this arrangement to an end and there were no further exports to the Japanese Army after 1917. But, like it or not, Harley-Davidson was inextricably linked with the emergence of the Japanese motorcycle industry; a fact which it certainly would have regretted had the implications been clear.

In 1922, the Murato Iron Works produced a copy of a contemporary Harley-Davidson. It was not taken up for production but, finding more success in producing motorcycle components, the Murato Iron Works evolved into Meguro Seisakusho. In the same year, Harley-Davidson's Export Manager, Alfred Rich Child, signed contracts to supply the Model J to Japan and, a year later, Child was nominated manager of the first Harley-Davidson dealer in Japan. In July of that year, he negotiated the purchase of 350 "big twins".

Sales to Japan remained important to Harley-Davidson in the following decade, with the 1,200cc VL V-twin finding particular favour with the Japanese Imperial Army. Civilian sales were also booming and, in 1932, Child signed a contract to supply blueprints, dies and machine tools to Sankyo Seiyako, a pharmaceutical company, who would produce Harley-Davidson motorcycles under the name Rikuo. It was intended that local content would gradually increase over a four or five year period. Some sources suggest that the machines were constructed by Meguro at their Shinagawa factory in Tokyo but, certainly, by 1935, the Rikuo was of 100 per cent Japanese origin.

After 1936 when the arrangement expired, Sankyo continued selling Harley-Davidson derived motorcycles, supplying to the Japanese Army from 1937 under the name Rikuo Type 97 – the "type number" indicating the year of development, 1937 (Year 2597 in the Japanese system). By the end of World War II, some 18,000 of these machines had been supplied for both solo and sidecar use, in the latter case, fitted with a three-speed and reverse gearbox. At this time, there were some 15 motorcycle manufacturers in Japan, but it would appear that only the Rikuo Type 97 was used by the Japanese Army.

In 1937, the Japanese Army had also trialled a four-wheel drive multi-terrain machine that was powered by a 1,200cc V-twin Harley-Davidson engine – or more likely, a Sankyo copy of a Harley-Davidson engine. It was approved for production but was never actually built in quantity, the five prototypes being all that existed.

Alongside the Rikuo Type 97, the Japanese Army and Navy were both enthusiastic users of motorized tricycles – known as *Sanrinsha*. These machines had first appeared

LEFT: **These Allied soldiers appear pleased with a captured Japanese motorcycle, almost certainly the Sankyo (Meguro) Rikuo Type 97 which was based on the Harley-Davidson.**

ABOVE AND RIGHT: **Produced from 1932, the Sankyo Rikuo Type 97 was the only motorcycle used by the Japanese Imperial Army during World War II; it was also available to civilian customers.** BELOW: *Abandoned Sankyo Type 97 at Balikapapan.*

in Japan in about 1930 for commercial use, and numbers of what was called the *Sanrinsha Type 1* (2601 or 1941) were supplied by Iwasaki and Kurogane.

After the end of World War II, Japan was banned from building passenger cars until 1949 but there was no such ban on motorcycles and Rikuo continued to build their Harley-Davidson copies into the late 1950s. However, it was one Soichiro Honda who changed everything when he purchased 500 military surplus two-stroke stationary engines and started fitting these into bicycle frames to produce a low-cost moped. In September 1948 he set up the Honda

Motor Company and the world of motorcycling was never going to be the same again.

Suzuki was established in 1952, with Yamaha following in 1955. Kawasaki started making motorcycles in 1960 after taking over the Meguro company who were producing a 500cc machine based on the BSA A7. By 1962, Kawasaki Motor Sales had been formed, the forerunner to the Kawasaki Motorcycle Company. Although these four companies have subsequently dominated the world's motorcycle markets, they came too late to have any significant effect on the military motorcycle scene, either in Japan or elsewhere.

Military motorcycles in neutral Europe

The total number of motorcycles constructed by the Allies during World War II was in the order of 541,000 – 425,000 were built in Britain, more than 106,000 in the USA, and almost 10,000 in the Soviet Union. For the other side, more than 277,000 machines were produced in Germany and Austria between 1939 and 1945, 18,000 in Japan, and thousands more in Italy. But of course this wasn't the whole story and military motorcycles were also produced and used by Ireland, Sweden and Switzerland, all of whom remained neutral during this period. Other countries, including for example Spain and Portugal, also remained neutral, but neither nation mobilized.

Ireland

Despite a proud rebel tradition and the boast of having been fighting the British for 800 years, the Irish Republic (Eire) is not a naturally militaristic nation. And, despite a single domestic motorcycle manufacturer – the Villiers-engined Fagan motorcycle having been manufactured in Dublin between 1935 and 1937 – neither does Ireland have an industrial tradition. Fagan had to close down by the time World War II, which Ireland always describes as "the emergency", broke out.

In 1939, the Irish Army comprised 7,500 men and, although Britain supplied some materiel and equipment, neither Britain nor the USA was prepared to supply more unless Ireland abandoned its policy of neutrality. De Valera kept Ireland neutral but the Irish

ABOVE: **The Irish Republic remained neutral for the duration of what was described there as "the emergency" but received military vehicles and other materiel from Britain. These BSA M20 motorcycles were supplied in 1940.**

Army eventually grew to 250,000 men and, although they were never particularly well supplied, among the equipment available there were 470 BSA M20 motorcycles that had come from Britain in 1940. By 1954, 372 of these were still in service, and many remained on strength into the 1960s.

Other motorcycles that have seen service with the Irish Defence Force (IDF) subsequently include the Kawasaki GT550, Honda 650 Deauville and Yamaha XS500. The IDF currently uses Suzuki DRZ400 machines, but the government has shown an interest in the RMCS/HDT diesel motorcycle.

Sweden

In 1939, Sweden was one of Europe's longest-standing neutral nations, having not been at war since 1814. However, while it must have helped that Germany was importing Swedish iron ore, the government recognized that a declaration of neutrality was no guarantee of safety, and the country had been re-arming since 1936. In 1937, the Swedish Army comprised 403,000 men, rising to 600,000 by 1945.

DKW military motorcycles had been procured from Germany but the government recognized that it would be better to employ

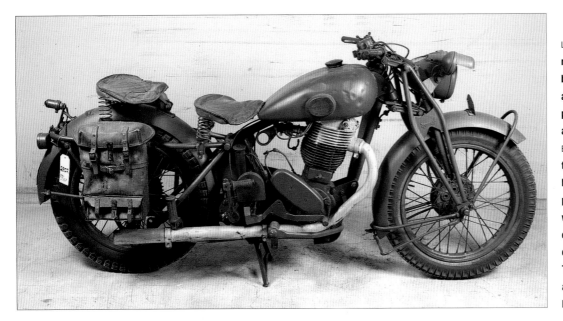

LEFT: **The Swedish M/42 was a rugged 500cc solo motorcycle built by both Husqvarna and Monark-Albin and was produced with both overhead and side valve engines.**
BELOW LEFT: **Dating from 1943, the Swedish NV M1000 was a heavy multi-terrain machine powered by an engine which was effectively two M/42 cylinders on a common crankcase.** BELOW AND BOTTOM: **The Swiss Universal A1000 was a V-twin machine intended for both solo and sidecar use.**

two new military-type motorcycles that were suitable for solo and sidecar use. Manufactured by both Universal and Condor in almost identical form, the machines were designated A680 and A1000, the former powered by a 676cc side-valve V-twin engine, the latter with a 990cc unit, and both were fitted with a four-speed Burman gearbox.

Both machines remained in service into the 1950s but were superseded by the Condor A580 and A750 from 1958, the latter also being manufactured by Universal.

domestic machines. Husqvarna had been the largest producer of motorcycles in Sweden during the 1920s and 1930s but by 1939 was committed to producing guns and armaments. In an attempt to solve the problem, the government approached Husqvarna to design a specialized military motorcycle which could be built by several companies. The result was the M/42, a 500cc, three-speed machine manufactured by Husqvarna, Monark and NV, with more than 3,000 built by 1945; two versions were produced, one with a side-valve engine and rigid rear end, the other with an overhead-valve engine and plunger suspension at the rear. The M/42 remained in service into the 1960s.

Switzerland

Despite being land-locked between Germany and Italy on two sides, and German-occupied France on the other, Switzerland was another European country with a long tradition of neutrality. Discretion generally proving the better part of valour, the Swiss Army, which was not mechanized to any significant degree, was mobilized on September 2, 1939, against the possibility of German invasion.

During the 1930s, the Swiss Army had used civilian motorcycles supplied by the Condor, Motosacoche (MAG), and Universal. While many of these remained in service during World War II, in 1943 the Universal company also designed

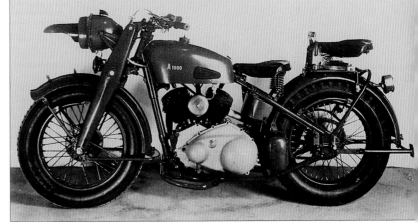

War surplus

When the war in Europe ended in May 1945, hundreds of defence contracts were terminated and the Allies found themselves with huge surplus stocks of every kind of imaginable item, including vehicles and motorcycles. Motorcycles that had further life in them – generally late models with low mileage – were retained, but thousands were put up for sale in the USA, Britain and across Europe as being surplus to requirements. Others were gifted to the governments of the newly liberated European nations.

In fact, the US government had actually started to dispose of large numbers of surplus motorcycles in the spring and summer of 1944. Among these were 15,000 Harley-Davidson WLAs, offered at a government-controlled retail price of $450; many were low-mileage machines which had never left the USA, some were even still crated. A quantity of shaft-drive XAs followed at $500 each. However, while this might not have been all of the surplus motorcycles that were available, US manufacturers were not faced with the situation of having to compete against their own products. It is said that there was an unwritten agreement between the US manufacturers and their government that, in order to protect the domestic market, surplus machines would not be returned to the USA from overseas.

The war had created considerable demand for motorcycles and, without having huge numbers of ex-services machines to depress the market, Harley-Davidson set about reactivating its network of franchised dealers and launching new civilian machines – albeit they were based on the militarized machines which they had already been selling to Uncle Sam.

ABOVE: **For the duration of the war, the major combatants continued to produce motorcycles in their thousands – Britain alone produced more than 1,400 machines every week between 1939 and 1945.** BELOW: **As soon as the fighting in Europe was over, enormous dumps were established where surplus equipment was collected prior to disposal.**

In Britain, the story was different. All of the Lend-Lease US-built machines, which had come from Indian and Harley-Davidson, were disposed of, and many of these found their way into the hands of UK dealers such as F. H. Warr, Marble Arch Motors and Pride & Clarke, where more than a few were converted to a more luxurious civilian specification. Unissued British motorcycles were generally returned to the manufacturers

LEFT: **Following the retreat of the British Expeditionary Force from France in May 1940, all available civilian motorcycles were purchased and stockpiled for military service.**
BELOW: **Motorcycles were stored in massive depots prior to issue or, in later years, disposal.**

as being surplus to the Army's needs and were reworked back to civilian form and offered for sale to the public through the normal dealer channels. Other, usually more heavily used machines were offered direct to the public through the Ministry of Supply auctions, often at rock bottom prices. Since civilian machines were both expensive and in short supply, there was no shortage of eager buyers. Spares were equally plentiful and the ex-military motorcycle provided cheap transportation at a time when the only alternative was to use the bus or tram, or buy a pedal cycle.

Although the large number of surplus machines offered for sale must have depressed the British motorcycle industry, surprisingly it was these machines which allowed the British manufacturers to gain a foothold in the USA. Norton started it all off with civilian-finished versions of the 500cc 16H, but Ariel, Royal Enfield, BSA and Triumph soon followed, all of them offering what were essentially ex-WD 500cc motorcycles with a civilian finish. Royal Enfield even managed to find a market in the USA for the WD/RE "Flying Flea". The British machines were comparatively light and powerful and stood up well against the heavy domestic V-twins of Harley-Davidson and Indian. Almost 10,000 examples were imported into the USA in 1946.

As regards disposals to European governments, the French situation sums this up well. In the late 1940s and early 1950s, alongside small numbers of essentially pre-war domestic machines, the French Army operated a mixed bag of British and American motorcycles. Cushman airborne scooters and Harley-Davidson WLAs and WLCs were used along with machines such as the BSA M20 and B-30WD, the Norton 633 Big Four, and the Royal-Enfield WD/CO. Other European armies had similar mixed inventories.

Germany, of course, was obliged to stop building military motorcycles as soon as the fighting stopped but nevertheless, many ex-*Wehrmacht* motorcycles found their way on to the civilian market.

World War II almost certainly contributed to the demise of the British motorcycle industry. The combination of shattered and worn out production facilities, continuing austerity conditions at home, and the ready availability of surplus military motorcycles meant that it was more than a decade before the industry showed any real signs of recovering from the war.

The immediate post-war years

At the end of World War II there was huge demand for cheap, utilitarian transport. Unlike the USA, the motorcar had yet to percolate through every level of European society and those domestic motorcycle manufacturers in a position to restart production found themselves with a ready market. It did not appear to matter that many were little more than a mixture of pre-war machines and wartime military models wearing a new coat of paint.

In Britain, despite the efforts of the *Luftwaffe*, the motorcycle factories had produced 425,000 machines during the conflict and, despite a ban on civilian sales, many of the manufacturers had survived. Civilian production was restarted almost immediately, but it seemed that those companies that had failed to secure substantial military contracts generally made little impression on the civilian market in the immediate post-war years, while a few never restarted production at all. For example, although the Brough Superior had been the chosen mount of T.E. Lawrence, the company supplied no military

motorcycles during World War II and, unable to resume production in 1945 because of a lack of suitable engines, had effectively closed in 1940, along with Rudge and Levis. Vincent struggled on until 1956, Sunbeam to 1957, with Scott and Excelsior barely surviving into the 1960s.

For others, the 1950s and 1960s were a time of plenty. British motorcycle manufacturers resumed their position as world leaders. But it was a false dawn and the impetus of those early years was insufficient to ensure long-term survival.

The demise of the once great BSA company provides a clue as to the fate of the post-war British motorcycle industry. One-quarter of the British motorcycles produced in World War II came from the huge BSA plant at Small Heath, Birmingham. The company launched the DKW-derived Bantam in 1946 and

ABOVE: **The British-built version of the DKW125RT was the BSA 125cc Bantam, a motorcycle used by the "Telegram Boys" of the GPO (General Post Office).**
LEFT: **The Matchless G80 "jampot" was firmly in the British tradition but could not save the company, which closed in 1969.**

LEFT: **Panther's iconic "sloper" design entered production in 1932, and the Panther-patented twin headlamps denotes this as the Model 100 De-Luxe. The Model 100 was put back into production after the war, using Dowty telescopic forks, but lasted only until 1963. The company closed in 1967.**

by 1948 was back in production. By 1951, BSA had bought the Triumph, Ariel and Sunbeam companies, and become the largest producer of motorcycles in the world with expansion continuing throughout the 1950s and 1960s. But BSA had underestimated the impact of the Japanese machines. Faced with dwindling sales the company, in 1972, merged with Norton-Villiers to create Norton-Villiers-Triumph. But, it was too late and BSA closed before the end of the year.

In Germany, the big motorcycle companies lay in ruins, often literally, as a result of the war. The Allied Control Commission, which was responsible for ensuring the Germans could not restart the production of military vehicles and equipment, forbade DKW, Zündapp, BMW and others from producing motorcycles until the growing Soviet menace led to the restrictions being lifted. Zündapp restarted production in 1947 with a 200cc two-stroke – a far cry from the massive machines of the war years – while BMW launched the all-new R-24 in 1948.

DKW, whose plants were split between the Soviet and American zones, put an updated version of the lightweight RT-125 back into production in 1946, but had to watch the model being produced in Britain, the USA, Japan, the Soviet Union and East Germany. NSU restarted production from their shattered factory with pre-war models such as the Quick and the OSL; they also managed to produce a number of *Kettenkrad* half-tracks for agricultural use. In 1949, their first post-war model was launched and, in the same year, the company signed a licence to produce the Lambretta scooter.

France and Belgium never managed to resume the volume production of motorcycles. Only Peugeot survived, with companies such as Gnome & Rhône, FN, Gillet-Herstal, Monet-Goyon, Terrot and René Gillet scarcely struggling on into the late 1950s or early 1960s.

In Italy, the post-war years were something of a boom time. The industry concentrated on converting ex-military machines for civilian use which provided breathing space to develop new

ABOVE: **The 500cc Sunbeam S8 was an attempt at producing a sporting motorcycle in the style of the heavy Sunbeam tourers. Less than 9,000 were sold over a period of eight years. BSA had purchased Sunbeam before the war, but closed the company in 1957.**

models. Moto-Guzzi, Gilera, and Benelli have all survived to the present day, and the post-war years saw some new companies established. For example, MV Augusta was set-up in 1945, at first producing a 100cc two-stroke but subsequently finding success with high-performance models. Laverda started producing motorcycles in 1949, again with a lightweight two-stroke, and scooters began to make an impact with Piaggio, Vespa and Lambretta all starting production in 1946.

Curiously, Japan was not perceived as a threat during these immediate post-war years. The country's industry was in ruins but, nevertheless, Honda started motorcycle manufacture in 1948, Suzuki in 1952, and Yamaha in 1955. It was the appearance of these machines in Europe that finally killed the once-great British motorcycle industry.

Isolated from the European turmoil, Harley-Davidson became the only US volume motorcycle builder when Indian collapsed in 1953 but, subsequently found itself struggling against British, and then Japanese, imports.

The Japanese "invasion"

At the end of World War II, Soichiro Honda purchased 500 military surplus two-stroke stationary engines and started fitting these in bicycle frames to make a simple low-cost moped. In September 1948 he established the Honda Motor Company and within 10 years had launched the Honda C50, a small 50cc motorcycle with a step-through frame, plastic leg-shields, and a fully enclosed engine and transmission. With its high-revving four-stroke engine, it was totally unlike other small machines of the period, and Honda set about breaking into a market sector totally dominated by the two-stroke models of other manufacturers.

But not only was the C50 unlike other similar machines of the period, it was also totally unlike the traditional British motorcycle and manufacturers such as BSA, Triumph and Norton, who were little interested in the bottom end of the market, failed to see the C50 as a threat. While it may not have been obvious at the time, the C50 was the start of the Japanese motorcycle "invasion". Having established a dealer network for their small commuter machine, Honda started to attack other market sectors and soon it was not just the bottom end of the market that the Honda wanted, it was the whole market.

The C50 went on to become the best-selling motorcycle of all time, providing cheap reliable transportation to millions across the globe. The machine is still in production today and has

RIGHT: **Suzuki's Power Free moped of 1952 featured a 36cc two-stroke engine and allowed the rider to choose between full power, pedal power or pedal assistance.**

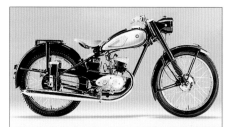

MIDDLE RIGHT: **Yamaha's first motorcycle, the YA-1, was launched in 1954, with just 125 examples built during the first year.**

BELOW RIGHT: **Having established themselves with lightweight reliable machines that were little more than mopeds, Japanese manufacturers quickly learned how to produce ever-more powerful and sophisticated products.**

TOP: **The Honda C50, or Cub, is the world's most numerous motorcycle, with almost 60 million built over 50 years.**
ABOVE: **In 1947, Honda started to market the A-Type, the company's first motorcycle.**
LEFT: **Honda's Cub F-Type dates from 1952.**

achieved worldwide sales of more than 60 million units. And where Honda led, Yamaha, Suzuki, and Kawasaki followed.

Within little more than a decade, the Japanese "invasion" had wiped out most of the European motorcycle industry and even managed to bring the mighty Harley-Davidson to its knees.

During the 1950s and 1960s, Britain had been a world leader in producing motorcycles, but by the early 1970s, BSA, Ariel, Matchless, Norton, AJS and Royal Enfield had closed down. Norton managed to re-open as a builder of powerful machines, and it was a similar story at Triumph where production ceased in 1983 and restarted at a considerably reduced volume in 1985. But as volume producers they were finished. In France, only Peugeot survived and, of the German giants, DKW closed in 1981 and Zündapp followed in 1985. Only BMW managed to hold on to its traditional luxury market.

Over in the USA, Harley-Davidson became the only domestic motorcycle manufacturer of any note when Indian effectively closed in 1953; but the company had been weakened by British imports in the late 1950s and early 1960s, and was purchased by the American Machine & Foundry Company in 1969. The company lobbied successfully for tariffs to be imposed on imported Japanese motorcycles, but there had been considerable damage done. In 1981, Harley-Davidson passed back into private hands as the result of a management buyout, but it took four years to reverse the company's fortunes and bankruptcy was an ever-present threat.

This turmoil in the world motorcycle market coincided with the European and American armies losing interest in operating motorcycles in significant numbers. So, while it is true that the sales of domestic military machines dropped during this period, there was no commensurate increase in the purchase of Japanese machinery and it could appear that the Japanese "invasion" had little effect on military motorcycle usage. This is not the case, and when military motorcycles started to reappear in the late 1980s, even the US military were purchasing

RIGHT AND BELOW: **With virtually no domestic motorcycle industry remaining in Britain, the 250cc Kawasaki KL-250 and KLR-250D8 trail bike has found favour with the British Army. The machine has also been used by US forces and has seen service in Iraq and Afghanistan.**

Kawasakis and Suzukis and the big Honda Pan European police motorcycle has proved popular with the British Army for convoy escort and military police duties.

Aside from small numbers of Armstrong/Harley-Davidson machines purchased by Canada and the UK, and small Peugeot trail bikes operated by the nationalistic French, the days of the European military motorcycle are gone.

In the end there is little doubt that the big four Japanese manufacturers have changed the face of military motorcycling, as surely as they changed the civilian market.

Diesel motorcycles

ABOVE: **The RMCS/Hayes M1030 is based on the Kawasaki KLR-650 and is produced in versions for the USA and Europe.** BELOW LEFT AND BELOW: **Details of the M1030.**

During World War II, both sides were forced into using a mixture of diesel and petrol engines in both logistical and combat vehicles. Clearly, this is far from an ideal situation since fuel transport and storage facilities need to be duplicated. Worse still, the volatility and combustibility of petrol also presents unnecessary hazards. It should be no surprise then that NATO has been struggling to standardize on a single fuel for more than two decades and, these days, even the smaller vehicles, such as Land Rovers, are now diesel-engined. The only non-diesel machine has always been the motorcycle.

While most people would baulk at the idea of a diesel-powered motorcycle, surprisingly, the machine has more than a 100-year history and diesel motorcycles have something of a cult following in civvy street. The Indian company Royal Enfield produced and marketed a diesel version of their Bullet model

until fairly recently. But sadly, the slow-revving nature of many early diesel engines hardly lends itself to the sort of performance most motorcyclists expect, and the fuel consumption is less of an issue than it is for car drivers. For this reason, the market has remained small and specialized.

However, perhaps unwittingly, the diesel-engined Bullet provided a starting point for the development of a specialized diesel-engined military motorcycle, which may be just what NATO needs to finally ban petrol from what, these days, they call the "battle space".

Back in 1992, Dr Stuart McGuigan and John Crocker of the British Royal Military College of Science (RMCS) produced a diesel-engined motorcycle demonstrator which they showed to the British Army. Their stated aim was to produce an engine with realistic power output and

LEFT AND BELOW: **The engine of the RMCS/ Hayes M1030 was originally based on the bottom end of an Indian-built Royal Enfield Bullet. The production engine is manufactured by Hayes Diversified Technologies in California, USA.**

performance characteristics, which would allow it to replace conventional petrol motorcycle engines.

The prototype proved to be both reliable and usable, and the RMCS claimed it would lead to the world's first production diesel-powered military motorcycle, but the College team experienced difficulty in finding a diesel-engine manufacturer who was prepared to work with them to refine the prototype. In the end, it was American money, appearing as a result of interest from the US Marines, which secured the future of the project, and the M1030, as it has been dubbed, became a joint collaboration between RMCS and Hayes Diversified Technologies (HDT) of Hisperia, California – Fred Hayes having been building specialized motorcycles for the US Marines for the last 20 or more years. US military interest also brought the British Ministry of Defence (MoD) to the table, and the development project ended up being sponsored by both the MoD and the US Marine Corps (USMC).

The production machine incorporates the chassis, transmission and some engine components of the Kawasaki KLR-650 (a standard dual-purpose trail machine) and is powered by a custom-built liquid-cooled, wet sump indirect-injection diesel engine. The engine will happily run on diesel fuel, aviation kerosene (AVTUR or JP8), and even rapeseed (canola) oil. Fuel consumption is said to be in the order of 50km per litre/ 140mpg giving a range of 650km/400 miles. The performance compares well to a conventional 250cc machine, with the 0–100kph/0–62mph figure, in just over 10 seconds, and a top speed of 130–145kph/80–90mph. And of course, the torque characteristics of the diesel engine reduce the need for gear changing which improves the rider's control across country.

A pre-production version was demonstrated to the press in May 2001, and the machine went into production, as two very similar variants, in March 2006, in California.

The success of this machine has also led to the development of a diesel-powered military quad bike by Roush Technologies using a Lombardini two-cylinder four-stroke diesel engine installed in a modified Arctic Snow Cat. Development started in 2004 and production was scheduled for 2006.

ATVs and quad bikes

It is doubtful that anyone would consider that the history of All-Terrain Vehicles (ATVs) – commonly called quad bikes outside of the USA – started with a Royal Enfield product dating from 1897, but that is certainly the case. In 1897, R. W. Smith, one of the financiers who had bailed out the original Royal Enfield company, built a quadricycle in which the engine was placed under the saddle between the rear wheels. The machine went into production in 1899 powered by a De Dion engine.

Alternatively, many might assume that the quad bike was developed by Honda but, in fact, ATVs were being produced in Europe and America a decade before Honda and the other

ABOVE AND BELOW LEFT: **Modern quad bikes first appeared in 1970 and, with their lightweight and all-wheel drive, have proved to be useful in many of the military roles once assigned to the Jeep.**

Japanese motorcycle companies joined the market. During the 1960s a number of US manufacturers offered small amphibious off-road vehicles that were were designed to travel across swamps, ponds and streams, as well as roads and cross-country tracks. In the UK, Crayford produced the Argocat and Cargocat vehicles from 1980, even producing a special military version. Typically constructed from a hard plastic or glassfibre "tub", these amphibious machines usually had six wheels or eight high-flotation wheels, all driven, and were skid-steered by either a wheel or a steering lever; suspension was simply achieved through the low-pressure tyres.

Honda produced what could be considered as the first modern ATV in 1970. It was a three-wheeled machine, clearly influenced by the earlier ATVs and featuring balloon tyres in place of conventional suspension, but it also borrowed heavily from Honda's motorcycle technology. The machine, which famously featured in the James Bond film *Diamonds are Forever*, was controlled in the same way as a motorcycle, the extra wheels providing stability at slow speeds, and the rider sat astride it rather than inside. By the early 1980s, proper coil-spring suspension had been introduced, using swing arms, and lower-profile tyres were fitted. In 1982, Honda introduced their ATC200E Big Red which, by including carrying racks, was effectively the first utility three-wheeled ATV.

Over the next few years both Yamaha and Kawasaki joined the market with high-performance two-stroke machines designed to

TOP, ABOVE AND ABOVE RIGHT: **Widely used by the British and US forces in Iraq and Afghanistan, quad bikes are fast, powerful and easily manoeuvred, and can even be used with a small trailer to enhance the load-carrying capacity.**

break Honda's monopoly, and the machines began to acquire a sporting image. Suzuki concentrated on four-wheeled machines, producing its first ATV, the LT125 QuadRunner in 1982/83. It was probably this machine which spawned the name "quad bike". In 1985 Suzuki followed this up with the first high-performance four-wheel ATV, the Suzuki LT250R QuadRacer which remained in production until 1992.

The 1986 Honda FourTrax TRX350 4x4 was the first all-wheel drive ATV and its success was such that other manufacturers followed suit and eventually the 4x4 drive-line became standard. At the same time, the three-wheeled machines were gradually discontinued due to safety concerns.

ATVs have proved popular with farmers and ranchers, hunters, and construction workers as well as with the sports fan, but it was probably the advent of all-wheel drive which encouraged military interest. Utility ATVs, which can reach speeds in excess of 125kph/77mph have become a popular mount for airborne and special forces operations, where vehicles such as the HMMWV or Land Rover are too large. The larger ATVs are able to carry supplies on built-in racks, and there are even 6x6 and 6x4 variants which have a cargo-carrying rear load bed. Some are even able to tow a small trailer.

Honda, Kawasaki and Suzuki have all supplied ATVs to the British Army; but the Japanese manufacturers do not have the market all to themselves. For example, Roush Specialist Vehicle Engineering has developed a diesel-powered military quad bike in association with Arctic Cat, and GHL Defence Products' Diablo diesel-powered ATV has been used as a mount for the medium-range Trigat anti-tank missile by the British Army's Infantry Trials and Development Unit. The vehicle has also been offered to the South African National Defence Force and is being considered as a potential vehicle for special forces personnel and

paratroops, also as a carrier for artillery and air-defence weapons. In the US, Polaris Industries have supplied 4x4 and 6x6 automatic transmission ATVs based on their standard Sportsman model to the US Army.

Crayford also continues to offer a version of the original 6x6 and 8x8 Argocat but since the appearance of three- and four-wheeled motorcycle-type ATVs, the earlier machines have started to become known as Amphibious All-Terrain Vehicles (AATVs).

LEFT AND BELOW: **Early quad bikes used balloon-type tyres for suspension and lacked all-wheel drive. Suzuki introduced their successful LT125 4x4 in 1982. Honda followed suit in 1986. The success of these machines means that all-wheel drive and independent suspension have now become standard features.**

Index

ACKNOWLEDGEMENTS

Picture research for this book was carried out by Pat Ware and Jasper Spencer-Smith, who have selected images from the following sources: JSS Collection, Warehouse, Getty Images, Topfoto, Imperial War Museum, Archives of Canada, BMIH, The Swedish Army Museum and Ullstein Bild.

A special thanks to Emily Fischer of the National Military History Center, Auburn, Indiana.

Much of the colour material has been supplied by the following (l=left, r=right, t=top, b=bottom, m=middle):
John Blackman: 13tl; 13ml; 52br; 56tl; 77br; 79t; 79m.
Andrew Morland: 14t; 15tl; 39t; 39b; 88t; 88bl; 89t; 89b; 92t; 92bl; 92br; 93t; 93b.
Phil Royal: 76t.
Simon Thomson: 2; 4; 5; 42–3; 48tl; 48tr; 52t; 52bl; 58b; 60t; 60m; 70tl; 70tr; 70b; 71br; 72b; 81t; 91b; 94b; 95tl; 95tr; 95ml; 95b.
World War One Society: 19t; 26b; 32b.

Every effort has been made to acknowledge photographs correctly, however, we apologize for any unintentional omissions, which will be corrected in future editions.

ABOVE: **German *Kradschützen* move through a Russian village during Operation Barbarossa.**